ESSENTIALS OF

Autoethnography

Essentials of Qualitative Methods Series

ESSENTIALS OF

Autoethnography

Christopher N. Poulos

 AMERICAN PSYCHOLOGICAL ASSOCIATION

The opinions and statements published are the responsibility of the author, and such
opinions and statements do not necessarily represent the policies of the American
Psychological Association.

Published by
American Psychological Association
750 First Street, NE
Washington, DC 20002
https://www.apa.org

Order Department
https://www.apa.org/pubs/books
order@apa.org

In the U.K., Europe, Africa, and the Middle East, copies may be ordered from Eurospan
https://www.eurospanbookstore.com/apa
info@eurospangroup.com

Typeset in Charter and Interstate by Circle Graphics, Inc., Reisterstown, MD

Printer: Sheridan Books, Chelsea, MI
Cover Designer: Anne Kerns, Anne Likes Red, Silver Spring, MD

Library of Congress Cataloging-in-Publication Data

Names: Poulos, Christopher N., author.
Title: Essentials of autoethnography / by Christopher N. Poulos.
Description: Washington, DC : American Psychological Association, [2021] |
  Series: Essentials of qualitative methods | Includes bibliographical
  references and index.
Identifiers: LCCN 2020028834 (print) | LCCN 2020028835 (ebook) |
  ISBN 9781433834547 (paperback) | ISBN 9781433834707 (ebook)
Subjects: LCSH: Ethnology—Biographical methods. | Ethnology—Authorship.
Classification: LCC GN346.6 .P68 2021 (print) | LCC GN346.6 (ebook) |
  DDC 808.06/692—dc23
LC record available at https://lccn.loc.gov/2020028834
LC ebook record available at https://lccn.loc.gov/2020028835

https://doi.org/10.1037/0000222-000

Printed in the United States of America

10 9 8 7 6 5 4 3 2 1

Contents

Series Foreword

Qualitative approaches have become accepted and indeed embraced as empirical methods within the social sciences, as scholars have realized that many of the phenomena in which we are interested are complex and require deep inner reflection and equally penetrating examination. Quantitative approaches often cannot capture such phenomena well through their standard methods (e.g., self-report measures), so qualitative designs using interviews and other in-depth data-gathering procedures offer exciting, nimble, and useful research approaches.

Indeed, the number and variety of qualitative approaches that have been developed is remarkable. We remember Bill Stiles saying (quoting Chairman Mao) at one meeting about methods, "Let a hundred flowers bloom," indicating that there are many appropriate methods for addressing research questions. In this series, we celebrate this diversity (hence, the cover design of flowers).

The question for many of us, though, has been how to decide among approaches and how to learn the different methods. Many prior descriptions of the various qualitative methods have not provided clear enough descriptions of the methods, making it difficult for novice researchers to learn how to use them. Thus, those interested in learning about and pursuing qualitative research need crisp and thorough descriptions of these approaches, with lots of examples to illustrate the method so that readers can grasp how to use the methods.

The purpose of this series of books, then, is to present a range of different qualitative approaches that seemed most exciting and illustrative of the range of methods appropriate for social science research. We asked leading experts in qualitative methods to contribute to the series, and we were delighted that they accepted our invitation. Through this series, readers have the opportunity to learn qualitative research methods from those who developed the methods and/or who have been using them successfully for years.

We asked the authors of each book to provide context for the method, including a rationale, situating the method within the qualitative tradition, describing the method's philosophical and epistemological background, and noting the key features of the method. We then asked them to describe in detail the steps of the method, including the research team, sampling, biases and expectations, data collection, data analysis, and variations on the method. We also asked authors to provide tips for the research process and for writing a manuscript emerging from a study that used the method. Finally, we asked authors to reflect on the methodological integrity of the approach, along with the benefits and limitations of the particular method.

This series of books can be used in several different ways. Instructors teaching courses in qualitative research could use the whole series, presenting one method at a time as they expose students to a range of qualitative methods. Alternatively, instructors could choose to focus on just a few approaches, as depicted in specific books, supplementing the books with examples from studies that have been published using the approaches, and providing experiential exercises to help students get started using the approaches.

In this book, Christopher N. Poulos guides readers through the fundamentals of autoethnography. Autoethnography involves a researcher writing about a topic of great personal relevance (e.g., family secrets), situating their experiences within the social context. Autoethnography thus requires deep reflection on both one's unique experiences and the universal within oneself. Dr. Poulos presents an exciting, innovative method that can be used to examine topics that are difficult to understand using more traditional quantitative and qualitative methods.

—Clara E. Hill and Sarah Knox

ESSENTIALS OF
Autoethnography

1 CONCEPTUAL FOUNDATIONS OF AUTOETHNOGRAPHY

When you first heard about autoethnography, you were skeptical. You are not alone. I have been reading and writing about autoethnography for over 25 years now, but for at least the first 5 years, I was skeptical. Then one day, I was hooked. Still, you might find yourself asking, "How could a researcher write about direct experience of the world, write reflectively, write from memory, write about social or cultural phenomena from a singular 'first-person' perspective, and call that research?" Can I really write about myself? Does that count?

But you keep hearing about it and wondering, and you have noticed that this way of writing qualitative research has spread widely, that this approach to social science research has caught on. There is even a 736-page *Handbook of Autoethnography* (Jones et al., 2013). So, you have become cautiously (or perhaps skeptically, optimistically, or enthusiastically) curious. To be sure, autoethnography is different than other kinds of qualitative research with which you may be familiar. Now you have picked up this book. You may even want to try your hand at this approach. My goal is to show you that autoethnography is a worthy endeavor. My hope is that this book will answer your questions about how to go about it and help you get started.

https://doi.org/10.1037/0000222-001
Essentials of Autoethnography, by C. N. Poulos

So, what is this thing we call "autoethnography?" In this volume, I trace the history, foundations, applications, aspirations, practices, agreements, and divergences among qualitative researchers who write about autoethnography. In Chapter 1, I set up the historical, contextual, and philosophical foundations for the method. In later chapters, I offer a guide to doing autoethnography.

WHAT IS AUTOETHNOGRAPHY?

Autoethnography is an autobiographical genre of academic writing that draws on and analyzes or interprets the lived experience of the author and connects researcher insights to self-identity, cultural rules and resources, communication practices, traditions, premises, symbols, rules, shared meanings, emotions, values, and larger social, cultural, and political issues. According to Adams et al. (2015),

> autoethnography is a qualitative research method that: 1) uses a researcher's personal experience to describe and critique cultural beliefs, practices, and experiences; 2) acknowledges and values a researcher's relationships with others; 3) uses deep and careful self-reflection—typically referred to as "reflexivity"—to name and interrogate the intersections between self and society, the particular and the general, the personal and the political; 4) Shows people in the process of figuring out what to do, how to live, and the meaning of their struggles; 5) balances intellectual and methodological rigor, emotion, and creativity; and 6) strives for social justice and to make life better. (p. 2)

Autoethnography—sometimes rendered as auto/ethnography or (auto) ethnography (Greek roots: *autós* = self + *ethnos* = people + *graphia* = writing)— arose out of field ethnography as a way to include the researcher's experiences and insights more directly into accounts of the scene being studied. Practitioners of autoethnography actively use writing about the self in social and cultural contexts to illuminate the contours of human social–cultural life practices. Like autobiography, memoir, and creative nonfiction, autoethnography actively and reflexively uses writing as an integral part of research and as a primary method of inquiry. In other words, autoethnographers invoke and use the discovery available in the writing process, using writing as a research practice that drives inquiry rather than as a "mopping up" activity after research is conducted (Richardson, 2005).

Grounded in active self-reflexivity, which "refers to the careful consideration of the ways in which researchers' past experiences, points of view, and roles impact these same researchers' interactions with, and interpretations of, the research scene" (Tracy, 2020, p. 2), autoethnography is a method that attempts to recenter the researcher's experience as vital in and to the research process. Autoethnography, simply put, is an observational, participatory, and reflexive research method that uses writing about the self in contact with others to illuminate the many layers of human social, emotional, theoretical, political, and cultural praxis (i.e., action, performance, accomplishment). In other words, autoethnography is an observational data-driven phenomenological method of narrative research and writing that aims to offer tales of human social and cultural life that are compelling, striking, and evocative (showing or bringing forth strong images, memories, or feelings).

Autoethnography involves the writer or researcher in crafting creative narratives shaped out of a writer's personal experiences within a culture and addressed to varied (mostly academic) audiences. Autoethnography is not identical to memoir, autobiography, or fiction—though good writers of autoethnography use some of the methods of the memoirist, autobiographer, and novelist (e.g., description, setting and plot development, pacing, rhythm, character development, dialogue, action) to advance the story.

Autoethnographers often rely on various methods of data gathering and research tools common to other forms of qualitative social research, including participant observation, interviews, conversational engagement, focus groups, narrative analysis, artifact analysis, archival research, journaling, field notes, thematic analysis, description, context, interpretation, and storytelling. They then craft compelling narratives that attempt to evoke and capture the lived experiences of the researcher (and coparticipants, as applicable) in relation to the phenomena under study. Most autoethnographers take a multipronged, layered, hybrid approach—drawing on various methodological tools common in qualitative inquiry—as they research social phenomena and craft compelling narratives about human social or cultural phenomena.

For example, in my book, *Accidental Ethnography: An Inquiry Into Family Secrecy* (Poulos, 2019), I take up an autoethnographic study of an important communication phenomenon in families by studying secrecy from a symbolic interactionist theoretical perspective (Blumer, 1931/1969; Cooley, 1909/1998; Goffman, 1959, 1963, 1967; Mead, 1934). I raised these general questions: "What are secrets? Why do we have them? What purposes do they serve?" (Poulos, 2019, p. 127). To get at these questions, I interrogated and integrated my personal experience; the literature on secrets and secrecy; the narratives and experiences of others as they connect with, talk about, and practice secrecy; and the general cultural attitudes that drive the urge toward secrecy—all juxtaposed to a prevailing U.S. cultural ideology that generally at least pretends to value openness and directness in communication (Philipsen, 1992). The resulting narrative draws on years of participant observation in a highly secretive family, along with interviews, artifact analysis, and narrative inquiry. The aim, in the end, is to describe, evoke, interpret, and critique secrecy as a family communication practice.

Similarly, in *Sweetwater: Black Women and Narratives of Resilience*, Boylorn (2012) wrote about the lifeworld struggles of Black women growing up poor in the rural South by weaving her life story into the multifaceted narratives of Black women of varying social statuses in her community. With her writing informed by close participant observation, interviews, participant narratives, and conversations, Boylorn developed a richly nuanced understanding of the resilience of Black women in her community of origin, offering an analysis grounded in Black feminist theory, critical theory, and narrative communication theory.

Boylorn's (2012) approach to autoethnography also highlights a rapidly growing interest in autoethnographic work that addresses identity politics. What she called "blackgirl feminist autoethnography" works from a particular identity standpoint to critique social structures that oppress Black women. Similarly, Adams (2011) wrote his story of coming out of the "closet," and Dunn (2018) wrote about lived experiences and representations of marginalized "White trash" (people of lower socioeconomic status) from her perspective as a member of that group. In recent years, autoethnographies focusing on the experiences of oppressed or marginalized cultural groups or individuals trying to make their way in the world have begun to emerge rapidly. Many of these texts are written as critical autoethnographies (see Chapter 6).

In sum, autoethnography is a qualitative research method used by researchers interested in narrative descriptions and evocations of the richly textured nature of lived experience. Autoethnographers seek to craft compelling tales that shed light on particular phenomena encountered in the research scene.

HISTORY

Beginning in the middle of the 19th century, anthropologists struck out into the world to study and write about "exotic" or "primitive" cultures. They pioneered the practice of *ethnography*—observing, writing about, and systematically analyzing people and their cultural practices—in the hope of constructing a systematic account or interpretation of culture that deepens understanding of the subject's lifeworld. Early ethnographers offered naturalistic "realist tales" (Van Maanen, 1988) that emphasized objectivity. These pioneers recognized and wrestled with questions of how to render textual accounts that would provide clear, accurate, rich descriptions of cultural practices of others.

The common approach among early ethnographers was to observe events from the perspective of an outsider looking in on the scene. But the project of becoming a "fly on the wall" was destined for problems because it quickly became clear that the locals were cognizant of—and adapting to—the presence of these "outsiders." Gradually, the idea of writing about the researcher's experience in situ (in position, as part of the scene) emerged as serious questions arose about the possibility and legitimacy of offering purely objective accounts of cultural practices, traditions, symbols, meanings, premises, rituals, rules, and other social engagements. After all, qualitative researchers are human actors—inexorably impacted and influenced by their responses to unfolding events and their cultural and historical premises, rules, and backgrounds—and yet they were expected somehow to be neutral or objective "scientific" observers. Many began keeping personal journals that were kept distinct from their research reports but were, on occasion, published as personal monographs or memoirs (Geertz, 1973; Lévi-Strauss, 1963; Malinowski, 1967).

As ethnographic research, pioneered by anthropologists, caught on and spread to sociology (and later communication studies and many other fields), practitioners of the method began to play around with what philosopher Gilbert Ryle (1949/1990) called *thick description*—a way of observing and describing human action and interaction that dug beneath the surface-level observation of human actors' behaviors (or thin description) and inserted commentary on, context for, and interpretation of these behaviors into the text. The idea was to delve into the deeper contours of meaning and context that animate that action or behavior. Of course, examining meaning making is a tricky and contingent business. In thick description, the author attempts to evoke a cultural scene vividly, in detail, and with care.

When the anthropologist Clifford Geertz visited Bali to study the cultural phenomenon of cockfighting, he found himself swept up in events in the village. He was clearly no "fly on the wall," dispassionately observing events unfolding around him. His account, published as an essay titled "Deep Play: Notes on the Balinese Cockfight" (Geertz, 1973), begins with a direct acknowledgment of how his presence was not only noticed by the islanders but also actually shaped how he could observe and participate in village life and what he was privy to. He immediately chronicled how he felt as an actively ignored participant–observer:

> We were intruders, professional ones, and the villagers dealt with us as Balinese seem always to deal with people not part of their life who yet press themselves upon them: as though we were not there . . . everyone ignored us in a way only a Balinese can do. (pp. 435–436)

As he gradually gained the villagers' trust (through shared hardship), however, his status suddenly shifted to a vibrant, engaged part of the interacting community, even as he was set somewhat apart by his "researcher" identity and "outsider" status. He also discovered (intuitively) that he had little choice but to use thick description to decipher what was "really" going on in the village. The villagers, of course, were knowledgeable human agents acting within their cultural milieu (Giddens, 1984) and were well aware—perhaps even more aware than Geertz—of how his presence impacted and even activated certain turns of events. Geertz and his wife (who was his research partner) were thrust into the middle of the action and were unable to ignore themselves.

The opening scene of "Deep Play" is often lauded—and used in courses on qualitative methods—as an exemplar of thick description. The writing is remarkable in that, unlike previous tales of the field, it reads in a visual-interactive "evocative" way, like a scene out of a movie. The notion is that carrying the reader into the scene through thick descriptive and evocative writing will lead to deeper understanding. Geertz (1973) went on to further champion and popularize this method of thick description for ethnographers in his essay "Thick Description: Toward an Interpretive Theory of Culture." Here, Geertz took issue with the minimalist and "menial" observations of his fellow anthropologists and argued that, at minimum, ethnographers owed their readers something more than mere "thin descriptions." As the story of Balinese cockfighting unfolded through Geertz's thick description, he turned his attention to the elaborate gambling ritual structures that animate the scene; his analysis makes sense of the cockfighting scene as a reflection of broader Balinese culture by parsing out how it animates social status.

Following Geertz, in *Tales of the Field*, Van Maanen (1988) cataloged three prevailing ways of crafting ethnographic narratives: (a) realist tales, which are attempts to offer an "accurate" and "objective" account of social action, "written in a dispassionate, third-person voice" (p. 45) and offering little in the way of researcher response to events in the field; (b) confessional tales, in which the ethnographer explores, in a personalized voice, his or her responses—so-called "self-data" (p. 73)—to whatever is at play in the field; and (c) impressionist tales, in which the ethnographer attempts a more figurative or metaphorical rendering of his or her participation-observation, with the crafting of "striking stories" as the primary goal (p. 101). In the 1980s, authors of ethnographic texts began experimenting with these more confessional and impressionist textual forms by crafting more evocative tales of research in the field, texts that soon came to be known as "autoethnography" (Behar, 1996; Ellis, 1995; Ellis & Bochner, 1991; Goodall, 1989, 1991, 1996). Most autoethnographers today write a kind of hybrid form of confessional-impressionist tale, generally crafting their stories in more performative, poetic, impressionistic, symbolic, and lyrical language than their predecessors in field ethnography but always focusing closely on the self-data inherent in confessional writing.

Driving the emergence of new forms of subjective (confessional, impressionist) autoethnographic writing, then, is the insight that the richness of cultural lives and life practices of others cannot be fully captured or evoked in purely objective or descriptive language. The researcher is both observer and participant in the scene. So, as ethnography continued to evolve, autoethnography—which dealt with the problem of researcher presence by inserting the researcher as the primary character and author of a story— emerged out of a need (driven by researchers' intuition of something missing) to capture deeper, richer, fuller evocations of cultural scenes. The exigencies of representation and evocation drove researchers. The need to "show forth" the world inhabited by the researcher as participant–observer— including the external social actions of cultural actors being studied and the inner emotional life and social responses of the researcher—drive the project of autoethnography.

Evocative autoethnographic writing (Poulos, 2016b, 2019) extends thick description to allow the author to construct research texts that conjure, arouse, or elicit vivid images, deep meanings, and sometimes intense emotions and thus shows the world and its actors in a richer, "thicker" way than simple realist tales can accomplish. As the autoethnographer digs through layers of symbol, action, imagery, ritual, meaning, and emotion, evocative autoethnographic writing evokes images, meanings, symbols, and emotions and explores the subjective positions and perspectives of the author as events, encounters, memories, actions, stories, and cultural practices emerge or unfold in the life of the researcher.

For example, a few years ago, I wrote about a suppressed traumatic childhood memory I had just recovered in a therapy session:

> That afternoon, I stroll out toward the sidewalk with my friend Howard. He's a smart kid, but a little lazy. He's one of those slow walkers. We amble up the street toward his house. Suddenly, a kid in front of us darts across the street.
>
> I look up, and hear the sick "thump!" as a car shatters his young body. There is blood everywhere. He lies in a twisted heap. His skull is oddly misshapen. One leg is askew, his foot sitting next to his head. So much blood! Then: Screams. The purest sound of misery I have ever heard. And then I see what—or really, who—he was darting toward. His Mom, who had been standing across the street, is now in the middle of the road, kneeling over his broken body, wailing. (Poulos, 2016a, p. 555)

In the article, titled "An Autoethnography of Memory and Connection," I interrogated and analyzed how suppressed and recovered memory functions and can impact daily communicative engagements. Making sense of traumatic memory recovered during writing and building clarity about its impacts in everyday life points the way toward a deeper understanding of the impacts of suppressed memory, as well as potential therapeutic applications of writing as a method of inquiry and, at the same time, offers a cautionary tale for those who are poised to engage in this kind of personal narrative inquiry.

By the late 1980s, it had become clear that the rich, textured, nuanced, messy, and dynamic world of human social praxis defies (or rather exceeds) an "accurate" (thin) description. Confronting a "crisis of representation" brought on by the emergence of postmodernist insights about truth and subjectivity and intersubjectivity (Denzin & Lincoln, 2005; Derrida, 1967/1974; Lyotard, 1979) and realizing that there is no overarching "Doctrine of Immaculate Perception" (Van Maanen, 1988, p. 73) that can guide them, qualitative researchers from various academic disciplines—notably anthropology, communication studies, and sociology—began widely experimenting with new and creative ways of rendering autoethnographic texts.

RATIONALE

A primary rationale for autoethnography is to engage the researcher's voice in qualitative writing. In place of an "objective" account of social reality, autoethnographers write from an engaged subjective position to get at the richer nuances of participation-observation in the social scene. To put this another way, autoethnographers seek to flesh out the lived, embodied experience of a researcher inhabiting human social–cultural spaces. By digging deeper into the researcher's experience, the autoethnographer attempts to offer richer, more complex, more evocative narratives of human social life. Furthermore, autoethnographers recognize that all social praxis researchers are embedded in the social milieu they are studying. We are all active, self-reflexive human agents.

Autoethnographic work is often interdisciplinary, drawing on insights from anthropology, communication studies, history, philosophy, psychology, sociology, theology, and other fields. The interdisciplinary nature of auto-ethnographic work facilitates the generative qualities of the narratives produced. It is in the intersections and overlaps between disciplines that much fruitful work can be done.

For example, in his autoethnographic narrative study of bullying, Berry (2016) brought insights from communication, anthropology, psychology, sociology, Buddhist philosophy, identity theory, and conflict studies to bear on a relational problem that too often leads to traumatic psychic and social ruptures for young people. He set up a new "wave" (p. 14) of bullying inquiry using autoethnography and personal narrative to investigate the impacts of bullying on both victims and perpetrators. Looking deeply into the stories of both victims and bullies, he concluded,

> The stories in this book demonstrate the relationship between communication and bullying, and the creative making and remaking of identity. This process of identity negotiation is a tensional process informed by social constraints, including stigma. As youth co-create "realities" concerning the practices of bullying and what it means to live through them, they also explore ways of understanding themselves and others. (p. 149)

This kind of interdisciplinary work and conversation, championed most prominently by Norman K. Denzin, founder of the International Congress of Qualitative Inquiry (ICQI) and editor of several leading journals featuring autoethnographic work (*Cultural Studies ↔ Critical Methodologies, International Review of Qualitative Research*, and *Qualitative Inquiry*), has facilitated synergy between researchers in over 30 academic disciplines and from over 50 different countries since the founding of these journals and at ICQI since 2005. Autoethnographers, as a group, want to take knowledge in a new direction—a phenomenologically grounded, performative direction, a direction that stems from an epistemology that sees knowledge as a form of praxis (action, performance, accomplishment).

SITUATING AUTOETHNOGRAPHY IN THE QUALITATIVE TRADITION

Qualitative social science and humanistic research, which is understood as a systematic investigation into and study of human cultural and social actions and practices, is the umbrella under which autoethnography resides. Ethnographers of all stripes (traditional, narrative, critical, auto-) engage in naturalistic inquiry, studying social settings, scenes, events, or other phenomena inductively, searching for themes, patterns, insights, meanings, interpretations, and explanations of human action and interaction.

Is autoethnography "science"? Perhaps the broadest meaning of that term—something akin to the German concept of *Wissenschaft* (which encompasses all kinds of systematic knowledge construction across the humanities and social sciences)—could be considered science. Most autoethnographers probably consider it closer to humanistic and artistic forms of research and writing (on a spectrum of humanistic and artistic forms of knowing to "pure" experimental and empirical science). Autoethnographers most certainly do not operate from a positivist or postpositivist paradigm of inquiry. The aim is not to make generalized or objective statements about the nature of reality.

Autoethnographers are not concerned with prediction, control, stability, or the generation of axiomatic knowledge. The practices of autoethnography are empirical and phenomenological—at least in the sense that the work is drawn from observation. But autoethnography is not guided by or grounded in measurement regimes (see Table 1.1 for a breakdown of what autoethnography is and is not).

In other words, autoethnography is particularly well suited to projects that involve direct participation by, and impact on, the researcher as a human actor in a scene or that involve personal memories, traumas, conflicts, observations, clues, and other experiences that need some unpacking. It is not suited for research projects that seek to generalize about groups of people, track trends, develop predictive models, construct axioms, or seek probabilities.

Autoethnographers seek to offer "rigorous, interesting, practical, aesthetic, and ethical" narratives (Tracy, 2020, p. xiv) by offering a grounded, subjective, hermeneutically informed and driven, local, socially constructed knowledge. Autoethnographers work from a reflexive standpoint and often take a critical-emancipatory approach to human social research. Autoethnographers, operating from an understanding of humans as knowledgeable agents who possess a measure of practical-moral knowing (Greek: *phrônesis*), seek to write accessible, engaging, clarifying, evocative, and open-ended texts; they strive to draw out implications, spark insights, raise questions, tell compelling stories, open conversations, inspire readers, move human beings emotionally, and create openings to further study and future research.

Autoethnographers most often draw from established ethnographic methodologies of data collection (i.e., ethnographic participant observation, field notes, narrative collection, interviews, informal focus groups, journal entries, and so on). In addition, autoethnographers work from and through the

TABLE 1.1. What Autoethnography Is, and What It Is Not

Autoethnography is	Autoethnography is not
Qualitative inquiry	Quantitative research
Phenomenological	Positivist or postpositivist
Focused on local knowledge	Focused on generalized knowledge
Evocative writing	Reporting
Interpretive or critical	Statistical
Suggestive	Predictive
Self-reflexive and subjective	Outer-directed or objective
Grounded in participation and observation	Grounded in quantifiable data
Driven by memory, story, experience	Driven by statistical generalizations or categories
Narrative, poetic, evocative writing	Research reporting
Seeking possibilities	Seeking probabilities
Written in first-person voice (generally)	Written in third-person voice

recovery of memory, close examination of personal trauma, systematic socio-logical and emotional introspection (Ellis, 1991, 2004), poetic and performative writing, family stories, explorations of identity and meaning, and everyday encounters and conversations.

But unlike many other methods, a primary focus of autoethnography is the writing process itself. As Ellis et al. (2011) put it,

> When researchers do ethnography, they study a culture's relational prac-tices, common values and beliefs, and shared experiences for the purpose of helping insiders (cultural members) and outsiders (cultural strangers) better understand the culture. . . . When researchers do *autoethnography* [emphasis added], they retrospectively and selectively write about epiphanies that stem from, or are made possible by, being part of a culture and/or by possessing a particular cultural identity. However, in addition to telling about experi-ences, autoethnographers . . . analyze these experiences. (p. 1)

Autoethnographers, as cultural analysts, take that additional self-reflexive step of systematic introspection and analysis to gain richer, fuller under-standings and interpretations of the phenomena under study. Thus, an autoethnography is not "just" a story; it is a story with a purpose—the prac-tice of cultural analysis and critique.

PIONEERS AND TURNING POINTS

As noted earlier, ethnographers began experimenting with autoethnography in the latter part of the 20th century. The call to write from a subjective, vulner-able, self-reflexive position—taken up as a kind of rallying cry for exploring the depths of the human spirit and as a way of approaching and writing research texts—was compelling (Behar, 1996; Goodall, 1996). An exact date is hard to come by, but early "cutting edge" work in autoethnography emerged in earnest in the late 1980s and early to mid-1990s. H. L. Goodall, Jr. (1989, 1991, 1996) began his trilogy of "new" ethnographic books by experimenting with autobiographical and autoethnographic forms of writing to explore the contours of human social life in organizational, group, and community settings. In the first book in the trilogy, *Casing a Promised Land: The Auto-biography of an Organizational Detective as Cultural Ethnographer*, Goodall (1989) crafted a narrative autoethnographic text modeled on the form and style of a Raymond Chandler novel, written in the second person, rich with thick description of place, time, and encounter. The text proceeds by placing the reader directly into the consciousness position of the autoethnographic detective or participant–observer-as-author as he wanders around a commer-cial organization and studies the communicative practices of actors in this cultural context. This experiment led directly to others in ethnography and autoethnography taking literary risks, seeking new and interesting ways to render research texts.

Meanwhile, Arthur Bochner and Carolyn Ellis (1992) began pushing the limits of systematic emotional–sociological introspection with their work on a personal struggle with a decision to get an abortion and with Ellis's (1995) groundbreaking book on personal loss, *Final Negotiations: A Story of Love, Loss, and Chronic Illness*. These works squarely confronted human emotions as raw, transcendent, messy, irrational, and sometimes ugly responses to the demands, exigencies, decisions, losses, conflicts, and traumas that come as part and parcel of the human condition.

Bochner (2001), in his foundational essay, *Narrative's Virtues*, responding directly to the emerging critics of the new autoethnography, laid out a strong philosophical and theoretical case for the crafting of narrative as a primary means of sharing and extending knowledge. Meanwhile, Norman Denzin's (1989) work in interpretive biography and Goodall's (2000, 2007) continued work in narrative ethnography opened the door for new generations of scholars to pursue narrative ethnography, autoethnography, performance ethnography, and other methods of qualitative inquiry that now fit squarely inside what Sarah Jane Tracy (2010) called the "big tent" of qualitative research.

Extending the philosophy behind autoethnography and performance ethnography in his influential book, *A Methodology of the Heart: Evoking Academic and Daily Life*, Ronald J. Pelias (2004) brought home deep insights about the practices and disciplines of everyday life as a writer–researcher in the academy seeking to engage the vulnerable heart, as invoked by Behar (1996). He wrote, "The heart learns that stories are truths that won't keep still" (p. 174). This is a clear clarion call for autoethnographers everywhere. Stories are, indeed, truths that will not keep still. And so, we write our stories to illuminate human social life.

PHILOSOPHICAL AND EPISTEMOLOGICAL BACKGROUND

Autoethnographers can trace their roots back to a range of philosophical and epistemological orientations in human social theory—notably, existentialism, phenomenology, narrative theory, and symbolic interactionism and social constructionism.

Existentialism

Emerging in the late 19th century, the *existentialist* movement in philosophy, beginning with Soren Kierkegaard (1849/1980) and Friedrich Nietzsche

(1968/2006) and extended by Fyodor Dostoevsky (1864/1994), Franz Kafka (1925/2012), Jean-Paul Sartre (1958), Albert Camus (1955), Martin Heidegger (1953/2010), Paul Tillich (1952), Walker Percy (1960, 1971, 1991), and others, rested on the insight that human beings are, as Heidegger put it, thrown into the world and left to carve out meaning from the raw material of existence. Epistemology, in existentialism, is grounded in the assumption of a "knowing" and creative subject, who engages a subjective praxis of action, performance, and accomplishment (including building "knowledge") in a dynamic lifeworld. The existentialist project is primarily one of crafting or carving out a sense of meaning in an absurd universe (Camus, 1955). As for writing philosophical texts, existentialists quickly recognized and exploited the enduring truth that meaning can be profoundly—and accessibly—crafted and expressed through artistic, literary, and dramatic philosophical works. Autoethnographers thus can find precedent in this stream of philosophical thought for the practice of working out ideas, cultural critiques, and insights not so much in treatises as in literary, narrative, poetic, and dramatic texts.

Phenomenology

Phenomenology overlaps, both historically and conceptually, with existentialism. Phenomenology, simply put, is the study of structures of experience, commonly thought to be organized through consciousness. According to phenomenological philosophy, consciousness is intentional, which is to say it is always conscious of something. Thus, phenomenology studies phenomena in the world, through the lens of conscious experience. Phenomenological insight is most often expressed, in writing, from the subjective or first-person point of view. Like autoethnographers, phenomenologists do not hesitate to write from their own point of view; in fact, they insist on it.

Narrative Theory (Narratology)

Narrative, in the sense intended here, "represents an umbrella term for forms of communication that have a) a sequence of events (beginning, middle, end); b) some sort of causal development between sequences that produces a conclusion; and c) memorable descriptions of events" (Boylorn & Orbe, 2016, p. 27). Narrative theory, as posited in the work of Walter Fisher (1985), proceeds on the basis of a few simple assumptions: (a) Human beings can be understood as belonging to the species *homo narrans*; we are, fundamentally, storytelling creatures—indeed, we are the only storytellers we know of; (b) humans experience life as a story (past, present, and future) driven by memory and action; (c) humans store much of our experience in the form of memories of stories; (d) humans are hungry for stories; (e) every argument is a story, and every story is an argument; (f) stories follow patterns; and (g) a story is the telling and showing of actions of significant characters across a span of time. These are the basic premises of stories. The task of the critical reader and the artful writer is to develop a comprehensive understanding of the narrative patterns and products available and then decide how to proceed, including which elements are most important to focus on.

Symbolic Interactionism and Social Constructionism

Meanwhile, in social theory, thinkers such as Charles H. Cooley (1909/1998), Herbert Blumer (1931/1969), George Herbert Mead (1934), and Erving Goffman (1959, 1963, 1967) were working out the implications of the theory of symbolic interactionism, which rested on the simple insight that the human self is a product of social, symbolic, and communicative interaction. Symbolic interactionists foregrounded the symbolic, collaborative, performative, constructive, interactive, and often ritualistic nature of social engagements between human agents. Researchers like Goffman used methods of analytical field ethnography to get at the deeper symbolic meanings of human interaction.

Ethnographers such as Hymes (1962) and Philipsen (1992) followed up, with an emphasis on exploring the symbols, meanings, premises, rituals, and rules followed by social actors. The implications of this theoretical breakthrough and its later developments and extensions in social constructionism (Berger & Luckmann, 1966; Gergen, 1992, 2009; Schrag, 1986, 1997; Searle, 1995; Shotter, 1993; Stewart, 1995) were not lost on autoethnographers attempting to reach beyond objective and realist constructions of texts. They quickly recognized the demand to account for the coconstruction of social reality in all human interaction (Bochner, 2001; Goodall, 1996; Pelias, 2004).

KEY DISTINGUISHING FEATURES OF AUTOETHNOGRAPHY

Several features distinguish autoethnography from other forms of qualitative research. First, autoethnographers actively engage researcher reflexivity, grounded in systematic introspection, bringing personal insight to the project of ethnographic research. Systematic introspection requires conscious attention to and focus on the researcher's experiences, memories, emotions, insights, epiphanies, and life practices as a way to gain a fuller understanding of the interaction between one's inner world(s) and the outer world(s) encountered in human social life.

Second, autoethnographers practice the craft of writing by engaging the methods and conventions of writers of fiction, creative nonfiction, autobiography, and memoir. Autoethnographers use, in the crafting of their confessional or impressionist tales, storytelling devices such as developing plot lines, scene setting, character development, thick description, dialogue, action, and dramatic renderings of social encounters. The aim is to write a compelling, striking, or even startling tale of self-revelation, self-evaluation, and human engagement.

Third, autoethnographers foreground the writing process itself as the primary method of inquiry. Autoethnographers write to discover, inquire, explore, and show rather than tell a reader what is known. Writing is crafted as social engagement and interpretation and critique, not a "mopping-up activity at the end of a research project. Writing is a way of 'knowing'— a method of discovery and analysis" (Richardson, 2005, p. 923). Autoethnographers use writing to learn about ourselves, our social worlds, our communicative acts, and our social engagements. Thus, the writing process is itself a form of inquiry, and this proceeds via close and systematic reflexive introspection aimed at discerning what might be going on.

Finally, autoethnographers

> seek to produce aesthetic and evocative thick descriptions of personal and interpersonal experience. They accomplish this by first discerning patterns of cultural experience evidenced by field notes, interviews, and/or artifacts, and then describing these patterns using facets of storytelling (e.g., character and plot development), showing and telling, and alterations of authorial voice. (Ellis et al., 2011, p. 2)

They often accomplish this by using an everyday writing, editing, and rewriting practice that operates as a method of uncovering truths that may be hovering just under the surface of consciousness. Writing is an exploratory practice; the notion here is that by writing regularly, the autoethnographer may uncover (otherwise hidden) truths by putting thoughts into concrete words. In the next two chapters, I address how to get started conducting autoethnographic research and how to begin writing compelling autoethnographic texts.

2

DOING AUTOETHNOGRAPHY

Design and Data Collection

In this chapter, I offer a clear, specific, step-by-step process for doing auto-ethnography as an integrated process of design and data collection. I outline specific steps in the process and illuminate those steps by walking them through an example from my research. For context, I am a scholar of communication in close personal relationships, with a strong emphasis on communication in families. I was drawn to this field of study by my own quirky (and sometimes dark) experiences of communicative dysfunction, violence, trauma, and secrecy in my closed family system. The example I discuss in this chapter is the practice of family secrecy.

OPENINGS

When I began teaching a family communication course at my university about 15 years ago, I focused my attention on communication patterns and practices in my family and to the communication patterns and practices of the families of my students and others in my community. I gradually became aware that secrecy and its concomitant cover stories, secrets, miscues, hints, innuendoes,

https://doi.org/10.1037/0000222-002
Essentials of Autoethnography, by C. N. Poulos

reversals, redirections, deflections, outright lies, avoidance maneuvers, and so on, can be seen as a common feature of family communicative life. Most families have secrets, and many family stories begin as secrets. What could be vibrant (and instructive) stories of infidelity, alcoholism, drug addiction, betrayal, trauma, grief, embarrassment, stigma, abuse, conflict, and so on, are often covered up or hidden from view, at least at first, by the forces of denial and secrecy.

Over time, such secrets eventually resist being held closely (Goodall, 2005). There is almost always a leak—or at least a bit of seepage. So, I began asking my students to collect family secrets as part of their semester-long research project (students write a family history book, including family stories, photographs, interviews, genealogical research, and so on). It turned out that nearly every family has a secret, and nearly every family also has a willing storyteller who is just waiting for a chance to spill the beans. After all, from a certain point of view, a secret is a story waiting for an audience (Poulos, 2019).

An autoethnographer wishing to write about a communicative phenomenon such as family secrecy would begin by carefully attuning his or her participant observation to the variations and permutations of secret keeping and secret revealing, searching ordinary conversations for hints, innuendoes, leaks, fragments of secrets; asking questions; conducting archival research using found journals and photographs; calling on memory; and stimulating storytelling in family settings. Following a systematic practice of participation, observation, querying, reflection, introspection, memory mining, story analysis, and exploratory writing, the autoethnographer works through the deeper contours of the phenomenon under study.

In my case, part of my journey of discovery about secrecy was engaged through intensive participant observation and construction of field notes, journals, and preliminary autoethnographic texts exploring the impacts of secrecy on my family life. Another part of my journey involved conversational exploration of the contours, meanings, and impacts of secrecy. The rest involved basic research, tapping into the narrative, philosophical, psychological, sociological, and communicative literature on the wider phenomenon of secrecy, with special emphasis on secrecy in families.

PRACTICES

Sometimes, as an autoethnographer of everyday life, I stumble on a situation during which a question or set of questions arises naturally or organically out of a communicative encounter. At other times, I go looking for something specific. I now offer a breakdown of how the process of constructing the research that led to the book began. The steps apply to any autoethnographic research project, though they may not always flow in the order presented here:

- engaging participant observation;
- attending to sense data and emotions;
- formulating research questions;
- conducting exploratory research;
- searching for stories, conversations, and artifacts;
- mining memories; and
- engaging in systematic reflexive introspection. (I address writing auto-ethnography in the next chapter.)

I now walk through each of these steps in the process, illuminating them with an example as I proceed.

Engaging Participant Observation

The first step to embarking on—and therefore designing and collecting data for—an autoethnographic project occurs while participating in and observing everyday life. One day during that first semester of teaching Family Communication, I found myself in an intriguing conversation with a student. I quickly became fascinated with the notion that people sometimes keep secrets from one another—even their closest loved ones—whether they are conscious of it or not. It was a small thing, but it triggered my curiosity. So, I became more attentive to the possibility of secrecy as a human communication phenomenon. The autoethnographer's practice here is to attune oneself to the phenomenon (or phenomena) of interest. The process I call *attunement* (Poulos, 2019)—what others call *mindful attentiveness* (Berry, 2016)—begins with noticing, in all communicative encounters, the variances in conversations that offer clues toward the presence of (in this example) secrecy and related "covering" communication phenomena.

As I enter the site or encounter; participate in a human phenomenon (e.g., communication); stumble into a moment of autoethnographic insight, observation, participation, or introspection; or work with a memory or an artifact, I become aware of my presence or consciousness as it relates to the subject(s) at hand. So, when I begin the practice of studied observation, participation, and introspection aimed at producing autoethnographic work, I seek to become fully aware of my presence. I work hard to center (or ground) myself so that I can gain a sense of mindful presence and attentiveness (attunement) as I attempt to gain insight into my driving research subjects, objects, and questions. Once I feel mindfully centered or grounded, I take in what is around me in the world or within my emotional, mental, memory, or spiritual land-scape, depending on my focus in the current work.

This process includes deep and active listening and close observation of words and other conversational clues, such as tone, volume, vocal variation, gestures and other body language cues, such as eye contact (or the lack thereof) and movement, and so on. It also involves monitoring and becoming attuned to my responses to my involvements and inevitably involves asking questions carefully, in a spirit of inquiry, to check and verify observations. At the beginning of the process, the search is for clues that something relevant to the subject of inquiry might be going on in any human encounter. As Walker Percy (1960) put it (through the words of his main character, Binx Bolling), I am on a conscious search:

> The search is what anyone would undertake if he were not sunk in the everyday-ness of his own life. This morning, for example, I felt as if I had come to myself on a strange island. And what does such a castaway do? Why, he pokes around the neighborhood and he doesn't miss a trick. (p. 13)

In other words, the autoethnographer is intentionally attuned to, conscious of, mindful of, and engaged in the unfolding events of his or her lifeworld (Poulos, 2019). As an autoethnographer, I am committed to poking around the neighborhood!

Examining Sense Data (Perceptions)

From time to time, I tune in directly to my senses to see what they offer in the way of perceptions in real time. What do I see, hear, feel, taste, smell, intuit? I strive to be fully present and aware of the data my senses are offering me. If I am seeking to understand and describe a past experience, I attempt to draw up these sense impressions as they reside in my memory and begin to build a sense of what it might have been like to reside in that moment in the past. Perceptions, as the phenomenologists point out, may not always be "accurate," but they do offer guidance (or at least clues) about our relationship to the world we inhabit. For example, even many years after her death, I can still remember the smell of my grandmother's biscuits baking in her kitchen. When I smell biscuits baking now, I am transported back to that kitchen and the fond nostalgic memories associated with my childhood visits there.

Exploring Emotions

I also work to become attuned to my emotional states (both now and in the past). A clear understanding of my emotional responses to life—especially when balanced in conversation with rational functions such as critical thinking—can help me formulate a clearer sense of the meanings of my human engagements. Humans are, by and large, emotional creatures. This is not to say that emotions should guide our actions. But they are ignored at our peril. It is also useful, in autoethnographic inquiry, to be attuned (as much as possible) to the emotional responses of other humans in my world—and my own.

Formulating Research Questions

Working with and from the raw data of participant observation, sensory input and memory, and emotions, I develop a question or questions I want to explore. Naturally, as a researcher, I need something to study, and I have to know the purpose and focus of my study. What am I trying to learn? What phenomenon or phenomena draw my interest, and why? Would closer study help to make sense of what I've noticed so far?

For example, suppose that, in the course of an ordinary conversation, someone reveals what was formerly a "big" secret (as my previously mentioned student did). Having already attuned myself to the possibility of secrecy, I might then decide that the communicative phenomenon of secrecy is worth exploring. This very thing happened to me one day, not long after my conversation with my student, when I discovered a photograph of my great grandfather. When my father saw me looking at this photo, and I asked him who it was, he (gradually) began to reveal a "dark" and long-kept secret about this man in the photo (his grandfather). So, as a result of this experience—and other similar experiences in other communicative encounters with other family members and later with friends, students, colleagues, and neighbors— I became even more attuned to the practice of secrecy as a common communication phenomenon. Over time, I determined that I wanted to gain a deeper understanding of the communicative phenomenon of keeping secrets.

At this stage, some preliminary research questions began to arise: What are the various kinds of secrets people keep? Why do people keep secrets? What drives or motivates acts of secrecy, particularly in families? What purposes do secrets serve? What are the long- and short-term effects of secrecy on families and family communication? How do secrets and secrecy shape the nature and function of specific family relationships? How do family secrecy and other forms of deception build harmony or create tension within the family communication system? How has secrecy impacted my life, the life of my family, and the lives of others and their families?

It is important to note here that it is a misconception that autoethnography is only about the researcher's life; as humans, we are always in contact with other humans. In that sense, my story is our story. But it is equally important to note that, as my observations continued, I began to foreground a more specific autoethnographic research question about secrecy that fundamentally changed the nature of the project: How has the practice of secrecy in my family of origin shaped my experience, my relationships, my memory, the stories I hold, my communication practices, the trajectory of my life?

As an autoethnographer, your research questions can be about anything you hope a storied, multilayered, qualitative approach to research might serve. Naturally, you should craft research questions that can and will (a) hold your interest; (b) hold an audience's interest; (c) present an opportunity to contribute to the research literature in your field; and (d) be explored in ways that writing about your responses to—and interpretations of—the phenomenon under study illuminates new truths about self, other, and culture.

Conducting Exploratory Research

Next, you will do some preliminary exploratory research into the possibilities engendered by your questions. As noted earlier, a big part of this process is simply paying close, mindful attention to the social phenomenon you are studying. And an integral part of that process is writing field notes, either during or soon after, an encounter, a discovery, or an event that may be worthy of further research. Taking detailed notes serves as "a record of what you observe, hear, overhear, think about, wonder about, and worry about" as you go about researching human social life (Goodall, 2000, p. 88). After my father revealed the potential existence of a family secret to me, I went home and immediately wrote in my field notebook about this particular encounter. My entry that day looked like this:

> I had an odd conversation with my father today. I was thumbing through an old photo album sitting on his kitchen counter, while I waited for him to go to the bathroom. I noticed that the photos were mostly of a time long ago, when my dad was a child—or earlier. The photos were not arranged in any particular order, or so it seemed. It seemed more likely that they had been somewhat hastily assembled into this album so that they could be preserved, but not chronologically. Many of the people in the photographs looked Greek, like my grandfather, though I did not recognize most of them. As my dad entered the room, I was staring at a particularly striking photo of a scowling Greek man wearing a suit and a fedora. The clothing made me think that the photo was likely taken in the 1940s. He looked like a Greek Humphrey Bogart. He was standing on a street corner, in what appeared to be the downtown area of a small U.S. city. The signs on the buildings were all in English.
>
> As my dad entered the room, I pointed at the photo, and asked, "Hey, dad—who's this guy?"
>
> He replied, "Oh, him? That's George."
>
> "George who?"
>
> "George Spiropoulos, your great grandfather."
>
> "Hmm. George lived in America?"
>
> "Yes."

"Hey, how come I never knew about George?"

"We don't talk about George."

At this point, he shut down, and changed the subject. It was clear from his expression (as well as his words and tone) that he did not want to talk about George. This encounter, to say the least, piqued my curiosity. I will definitely pursue the matter, though it appears that my dad doesn't want to talk about it. I have my work cut out for me. (Poulos, 2019, pp. xvi–xvii)

As I waited to have another conversation with my dad, I thought about what might have been going on. I wrote reflexively about how this seemingly innocuous random conversation affected me and about my dad's approach to shutting it down, admittedly speculating about why he may not have wanted to talk about George. Frankly, I wondered what the big secret could be and why he was still resisting talking about his grandfather—who, by my reckoning, must have died at least 50 years earlier. I was curious.

So, to add texture to the unfolding puzzle, I began reading up on the phenomenon of secrecy, with a particular emphasis on family secrets and practices of secrecy. I reread Goffman's (1959, 1963, 1967) extensive work on stigma, face work, and impression management. I read the literature on codependency and denial (Black, 1985, 2002; Bradshaw, 1995). I read Kuhn's (1995) sociological study of family secrecy. I hunted down every article, book, and study I could locate. I even read novels and poems that focused on family secrets to focus on how secrets are represented in our broader culture. I began to catalog a list of readings that would serve my project. At this stage, it occurred to me that I had found some research questions that might bear some fruit. I had also cataloged a body of literature that could be brought in later to frame and interpret the writing, to link the research to the larger body of inquiry relevant to the project at hand. In this way, autoethnographers enter an ongoing conversation about human social phenomena.

Searching for Stories, Conversations, and Artifacts

Next, you will continue paying even fuller and more careful attention to encounters, conversations, relationships, stories, and artifacts related to your phenomenon. In this stage, it is useful to ask for stories, pose focused but open-ended conversational questions, and closely examine any bit of information or object that emerges in response to your queries. You may also conduct informal interviews or simply ask others to reveal what they know that may be relevant.

At this point in my study of secrecy, I decided I was indeed onto something. The evidence was mounting. Secrecy, it seemed to me, could be read as a vibrant and underexplored communication phenomenon that served potentially vital (positive and negative) purposes in family communication. Informally, I decided to bring up the subject of family secrecy in as many conversations with as many people as I could. Sometimes, I was shut down or deflected. But I operated from the assumption that, if pressed, people would "cough up" the secret or at least reveal their opinions and insights about the practice and purposes of secrecy. I was persistent. I asked my students to be persistent, as well. Indeed, it turned out that my most persistent students, sent home with the assignment to discover a family secret, could almost always find someone who was just waiting for the opportunity to convert the secret into a story. This was encouraging.

As I pressed my dad about George, I finally said, "Come on, Dad. It's been over 50 years. Isn't there a statute of limitations on secrets like that? I mean, nobody who knew him—not one of the players in that scene—is even still alive, except you! You're it. What could he possibly have done that was so bad we can't talk about it now?" Somewhat begrudgingly, my dad spilled the beans that day. It turned out to be a simple story of family abandonment. Clearly, it was one that powerfully shaped my family, however. Greeks never forget. My great grandfather came from Greece to America to pursue the American dream. He planned to earn his fortune and send for his family in Greece. My father told me about George, a story that was later corroborated by a cousin in California:

> "Uh, I guess the story goes that he sort of abandoned his family in Greece."
>
> "Really? What happened?"
>
> "Well, I think he left his wife, my grandmother, when she was sick, left her in the care of Pop's sister. Apparently, he came to America and never contacted them again."
>
> "Wow. That's harsh."
>
> "Yeah, Pop was furious at him. I think George followed Pop here. I mean, Pop came first and then his dad came. They were in contact at first, but when Pop found out what had happened, he refused to speak to his father again. He never talked about him, either. As far as I know, my grandfather moved to California. Then, when he died, Pop got a call, asking what should be done with the body. Pop told them, 'Bury him.' That was it. But he forbade us even mentioning George, threatening to disown us if we did." (Poulos, 2019, xvi–xvii)

As I delved deeper into this story and secrecy more generally, I continued to write in my field notes. I learned, observed, and participated in family life, and I continued to wonder, wander, dig, ask, and write about it all—and the contours of family secrecy began to take shape. I searched and read all the literature that seemed even remotely relevant to what I was hearing and observing. I wrote reflexively about my impressions of what might be going on, and I attempted some preliminary interpretations. For example, as I heard more, I began to wonder further about the power of stigma and face and impression management as social forces that encourage or suggest secrecy as a viable option, while at the same time wondering and writing about what it would be like to live in a family where communication was more fully open.

Along the way, I became acutely aware of how secrets shift depending on the point of view and life experiences of the teller.

I also examined the artifacts my family members, friends, students, and other interlocutors produced in response to my inquiries about family secrets and secrecy practices. It was somewhat surprising how often an artifact that could easily have served as a revelatory mechanism but most often was kept under wraps suddenly emerged in these conversations. These artifacts included genealogical research (my California cousin sent me a family tree that included information about my great grandfather); collected but suppressed newspaper accounts (a student produced family news stories—about a murder—that were later converted to dark family secrets and kept in a secret box in an attic); photographs; contents of attics, basements, and closets; and journals, diaries, letters, and other household objects. Every artifact produced in these conversations had a secret attached to it—a secret now converted to a story, ready for examination.

Mining Memories

Along the way, as an autoethnographer, you should pay close attention to your memories related to the phenomenon under study. I began to examine my memories of secrets and secrecy and to explore (in writing) any memories— or gaps in memory—that emerged as I worked through the data. Indeed, autoethnographers often examine memory as a primary data set. As an intro-spective and reflective method, autoethnography relies heavily on memory as a pathway to a deeper understanding of the human condition. In addition to writing to come to grips with present experiences, autoethnographers engage in retrospective sense making by mining the storehouse of individual and collective memory. This is not to say that memory is thought to be an accurate representation of precisely how events unfolded in the past. Rather, memory is a primary tool of human sense making and meaning making that helps us construct a coherent story of our lives.

Indeed, if you read autoethnographic literature widely, it will quickly become clear that a primary form of data for the autoethnographer is memory. Memory builds a human's sense of coherent identity and is a fundamental building block of human narrative reality. I will never forget a student who, on the first day of my autoethnography class (in which I emphasize memory as a crucial form of data), raised her hand and said, "I'm not sure I should be in your class. You see, when I woke on my 16th birthday, I had no memories of anything that had happened before that day. I don't have much to work with." It turned out that she had experienced some sort of fever-induced total amnesia. She was, now 5 years after that birthday, still struggling to piece together her past and her sense of who she was and where she came from.

Of course, I encouraged her to stay. And she started her story with her earliest memory—waking up on that fateful morning—and crafted a truly striking tale about the quest for recall, the longing for memory, the need for memory as a sense-making tool, and about how those of us who are blessed with memory have something she does not—a sense of how she got to where she is now. Two years later, she was our commencement speaker, and she spoke of how her work with autoethnography was an important part of her reconstruction journey.

In my research on family secrecy, I recovered a memory of one of my little dark secrets from childhood—anxiety-driven bedwetting, which I went to great lengths to conceal, including learning how to do laundry and secretly and quietly doing it as necessary in the middle of the night as early as age 5. So, we autoethnographers take memory seriously, even as we are aware of its slippery vicissitudes, shadowy fragmentations, and potential wrong turns. The autoethnographer digs through, sifts, sorts, and mines the meanings of memories as they rise into consciousness or emerge in story or dialogue. Of course, this kind of memory meaning is *interpretive* (subjective and open to various explanations); memory is not, for most of us, *eidetic* (precise recollection). Rather, memory is more often part of our way of seeing how our lives are pieced together, of making sense of our experience. For the autoethnographer, as for most humans, memory is one of the primary cognitive tools for constituting or cultivating a sense of being grounded in time and space, while at the same time building the story of a life, which is constituted of a past, a present, and a hoped-for future (May, 1991; McGlashan, 1986, 1988).

Engaging in Systematic Reflexive Introspection

Continuing my research, I work to reach outward (beyond myself) and inward (within my consciousness) to get at some of the deeper contours of my experience. In reaching out beyond myself, I try to gather as much information as possible about what is going on through continued observation, direct participation, conversation, and thick description of the site or phenomenon under study. This move requires writing (in field notes, journals, partial texts) as I go along, offering detailed descriptions of people, places, events, encounters, artifacts, and experiences across the *durée* of time (over long periods of life). Who are we in this space, this time, this moment? What are we up to? Here I strive to understand how space, time, people, events, encounters, memories, emotions, and actions intersect, overlap, and create meaning.

I engage as an active participant in everyday life while striving to observe human life with clarity and focus, bringing my life experience into play in the process of observation and participation. I seek to be an ultra-absorbent, new, improved autoethnographically inclined and informed human sponge. I focus and absorb. At this stage, I tend to write down everything I see, hear, smell, taste, touch, remember, feel, connect with, and intuit. I especially continue to write down (in my field notes) everything I hear or overhear, what people say and do, how people move about and engage with each other, and any encounters I observe or experience.

As an inherently introspective, reflexive, and retrospective method, autoethnography is deeply grounded in embodied experiential knowledge generated through intentional self-reflexivity and awareness. As such, some scholars may see it as "biased." It is, in fact, biased—in favor of a world view that embraces a practice of qualitative inquiry as a subjective, participatory, personal, local, self-reflexive, generative praxis aimed at evoking, interpreting, and critiquing human social life. It is biased in favor of a view that the studied insights of an engaged researcher have value. It is biased against the notion that humans can ultimately attain objectivity.

But it is not as simple as just writing from one's point of view. Many young scholars think it will be easy to write an autoethnography, but they are soon disabused of this notion. Good autoethnography requires mindful and studied observation of and participation in human social life, deep reflection and systematic introspection, emotional and attentive attunement, continuous self-reflexivity, thoughtful attention to theoretical and philosophical constructs and concerns, grounded cultural and historical knowledge, educated speculation and interpretation and cultural critique, and serious attention to the craft of writing. Like all qualitative inquiry, it must pass through rigorous peer review—and to do so, it must contribute to knowledge while also being evocative, compelling, moving, generative, dialogical, and transformative (see Chapter 6). The autoethnographer crafts unique texts to add to the coconstruction of a deeper understanding of our socially constructed realities.

As I look back reflexively into my consciousness to engage in building a systematic understanding and thick description of my emotional responses, I reflect and ask: Who and where am I in all this? What do I bring to this place, event, culture? What is my heart telling me? What emotional and other affective responses do I feel? What are the connections between my thoughts, senses, memories, emotions, and experiences? Who am I here and now? How do I feel? What is my intellectual and emotional response to the situation at hand or the memory that is arising or the artifact I've stumbled on in my search? This is how I, as an autoethnographer, "collect data." In the next chapter, I attempt to demonstrate how to accomplish all that by using writing as a method of inquiry.

3

WRITING AUTOETHNOGRAPHY

In this chapter, I explore the processes and practices of writing autoethnography as a focused method of inquiry and interpretation. It is my hope that I can show aspiring autoethnographers a clear pathway to writing high-quality autoethnographic texts. To help me accomplish this mission, I write my way through two examples. The first example is about the "flow" of the writing process, where the writer allows the writing to go where it pulls you. The call from this example is to follow the inspiration—the spark of creativity—that lives within the writing process. The second example is more concretely about focusing autoethnographic writing on a topic that has been a central part of my research as a family communication scholar: father–son relationships. Both are illustrative of how the process of writing-as-inquiry can unfold through a balance of structure and improvisation.

WRITING AS A METHOD OF INQUIRY

From time to time, I "retreat" from participation and actively reflect, via focused writing, on the lived experience of observation, participation, dialogue, and action. What is going on here? I offer questions, variations, possibilities,

https://doi.org/10.1037/0000222-003
Essentials of Autoethnography, by C. N. Poulos

interpretations, feelings, and openings to new ways of seeing and experiencing the site, culture, and space. I try to draw back and see the experience from outside it. Then, as I write, I continue to engage in systematic reflexive introspection, driven by the writing process, searching for insights derived from action and encounter, aimed at coming to grips with what is going on in this lifeworld I inhabit.

Autoethnographers use active writing as a way to clarify and make sense of human experience. Autoethnography is a particularly salient approach for attempting to understand the rich but messy emotional–social lives of members of human communities, including the researcher her- or himself, especially when exploring such fundamentally personal questions as shown in my example: How has secrecy impacted my life, the life of my family, and the lives of others and their families? If I chose to explore this phenomenon through another method, I might focus only on the latter part of that question. But autoethnography opens the door for me to include my experiences in the research in ways that other methods do not.

In many ways, autoethnography is as much an approach to living life as it is a research method—it is a way of life (The Ethnogs et al., 2011). An autoethnographer adopts autoethnographic inquiry as a way of life, and what ensues is a complex and captivating struggle to come to grips with the meaning(s) of human social interaction. The researcher engages in a search for meaning, understanding, sense making, insight, knowledge, coconstruction of social reality, and evocation—in written story form—of our rich, textured, nuanced, complex, embodied human experience. Much of this is accomplished through disciplined practices of writing and rewriting.

So, most autoethnographers write every day, using writing as a method of inquiry and reflexive research practice. The writing process is a search for meaning, making sense, and moving from the raw data of observations, conversations, artifacts, and memories to a coherent research-constructed story-text. The practice is one of crafting a story that will draw your reader into your world; examine a phenomenon or phenomena through thick description, action, dialogue, character development, and plot construction; and build an emerging interpretation of it all.

Autoethnographers use writing as a primary method of inquiry (Richardson, 2005), crafting stories that evoke the deeper contours of the author's embodied, emotional, intellectual, and spiritual life in response to—and as commentary, interpretation, and critique of—the events, phenomena, and structures of human social contexts (Poulos, 2019). In other words, as humans do with all other life engagement, autoethnographers learn by writing. The writing itself is an integral part of the process of investigation and discovery, not a closing off or ending practice. So, autoethnographers do not approach writing as a final stage of research, with an attitude of "writing up results" after research is conducted. Rather, writing is central to the research process throughout the life of a study. Every autoethnographer hopes to craft compelling emotional, intellectual, spiritual, embodied and performative, and social and dialogical writing and to stimulate equally emotional, intellectual, spiritual, embodied reader responses to the work.

Autoethnographers, by design, attempt to write this way to reach into research questions in ways that other methods cannot. Of course, any research project can take up any method that fits the questions at hand, and questions can be reconfigured to match particular methods of inquiry. But as noted in Chapter 1, autoethnography is particularly well suited to projects that involve direct participation by, and impact on, the researcher as a human actor in a scene or that involve personal memories, traumas, conflicts, observations, clues, and other experiences that need some unpacking. Autoethnography is a direct attempt to bring the participation, attention, and reflexivity of the knowledgeable researcher, as a human agent, into the center of the research scene to get at meanings that cannot be grasped objectively (from a distance). Autoethnographers probe and mine the personal and relational meanings of everyday observations of human social life, conversations, memories, stories, and artifacts that are, in the researcher's judgment, worthy of study.

So, as noted in Chapter 2, the autoethnographer is deeply involved, daily, in poking around his or her "neighborhood" (area of research interest or focus), hanging out and observing, participating, communicating, and most important, writing about what it means to be a human being among other human beings on this earth—or at least what it is like to be this human being among others. Autoethnographers do not flinch from performing writing as the primary method of inquiry; indeed, we embrace it. We insist on writing as a dynamic, fluid, continuous method of inquiry.

Autoethnographers explore the contours, complications, and fascinations of human social life through daily practices of observing, participating, journaling, field note taking, engaging in dialogue, questioning, and living the writing life as a method of inquiry. We read signs and try to decipher their meaning (Goodall, 1996; Pelias, 2004). We read actions and attempt to understand their impacts. We read the human social world and work to engage it via active writing practices. What drives autoethnographic writing is a curious fascination, an embracing of the mystery that swirls around us as we try to come to grips with what it means to be a human being (Goodall, 1996; Marcel, 1960; Merleau-Ponty, 1962; Otto, 1958; Percy, 1960, 1971, 1991). With this fascination—wedded to and integrated with the ever-increasing store of practical, moral, cultural, historical, literary, and scientific knowledge the autoethnographer brings to the table—the autoethnographer writes to explore, discover, integrate and synthesize, analyze, interpret, and craft a compelling story. We place our writing into conversation with the literature already in play in our field of study, and we use that work of other scholars to inform, enhance, shape, and challenge our views, perceptions, and perspectives. We may also challenge other scholarship, calling some approaches and conclusions into question.

Thus, the practitioner of autoethnography approaches writing as a craft, a careful and practiced "making" of narrative texts. Autoethnographers activate what Ellis (2004) called "The ethnographic I" (p. 1) in a writing praxis that proceeds through both unstructured and systematic reflexive introspection. So, as noted in Chapter 2, the research "design" is a design of participation–observation and writing-as-inquiry and daily learning–writing praxis, a making of human knowing that enters into the long chain of utterances that is the story of human dialogue (Bakhtin, 1993).

ASSUMPTIONS

The autoethnographer strives to craft a striking tale that links the data of lived experience to the broader sociocultural conversation about what it means to be human and then links all that to the literature of an academic discipline or disciplines in some meaningful and theoretically sound way. The following are some basic assumptions about research-driven autoethnographic story writing that speak to the logic, motivations, and structures of story.

Stories Are Active

Compelling stories are about people (characters) taking action in particular places over a recognizable period (plot). Good stories are about characters coming and going, engaging and disengaging, hitting obstacles and overcoming them, running into and working through conflicts, and moving through space, time, and relationships. But they are more than all that. Good stories speak to the heart and the mind of the reader and into the heart of what it is to be human. Making good stories is what we humans do, how we make sense, how we go on in life. Stories are at the core of our social being. We humans are, fundamentally, story makers, storytellers, and story consumers. We are, as Walter Fisher (1985) pointed out, *homo narrans*.

Stories Follow Certain Structural Conventions

Autoethnographers often use standard narrative paradigms to guide the structure of their work. In the classical narrative paradigm, a protagonist meets a challenge (antagonist) or conflict, and action rises along a timeline until the action reaches a climax, followed by resolution or denouement. Another common archetypal structure of the autoethnographic text loosely follows what mythologist Joseph Campbell (1949) called "the hero's journey." The central subject (hero) of an autoethnographic study patterned after the hero's journey is the "ethnographic I" (Ellis, 2004, p. 1) of the researcher, who operates as a protagonist-hero facing obstacles, traumas, conflicts, dreams, losses, emotions, memories, puzzles, conundrums, and befuddling interactions while proceeding through daily life. Along the way, the protagonist-hero encounters both foes (obstacles or challenges) and companions (helpers) and, in the end, more often than not, overcomes or at least meets those challenges and, triumphant or wounded or both, returns to the community with a gift: a story of struggle—and, possibly, of redemption. Or at least a partial story. Other autoethnographic texts take a more postmodern, poetic, or impression-istic story form, seeking to deconstruct, reconstruct, or show cultural practices from a critical, sometimes fragmented, often incomplete perspective—thus mirroring the often-unsettled nature of life itself.

Stories Tap Into the Improvisational Nature of Creative Writing

Balancing the emphasis on narrative structure is the creative "juice" of a story, which comes from tapping imagination, intuition, and the flow of improvi-sation. The analogy of jazz music can serve as an illustration of how this works. Jazz musicians follow clear conventions, playing recognizable songs with a well-structured configuration of notes. At the same time, built into the "structure" of jazz is the embedded practice of purposeful improvisation, in which each musician is offered opportunities to improvise playful "riffs" on the song. These riffs follow the rules of jazz, but they are made up on the spot in the spirit of the moment and in response to the song, the audience, and the energy of the band (Eisenberg, 1990). Similarly, autoethnographic storytellers build on the conventions of standard narrative paradigms while also improvising or "riffing" creatively in the telling or showing of storied action (see the following examples).

Stories Are Provocative

Compelling stories evoke, provoke, and stoke the fires of being and are often intended to spark action, change minds and hearts (persuade), offer some sort of "moral," or speak to insights and lessons that transform our collec-tive thinking. They make claims but not in the "usual" sense of that word. These claims are demonstrations or manifestations of truths—inner truths and outer truths—all with a touch of evocative resonance, intended to provoke dialogue.

All Research Is Storytelling

Research and story come together (converge) as you search for clues and use active writing-as-inquiry to make sense of what you are seeing, noticing, experiencing, feeling, remembering, and thinking. Even highly scientific research reports tell a story that has to be digested, understood, and integrated into the consciousness of the reader. If a writer (of anything) wants a reader to come to grips with the gist, moral, punch line, conclusions, speculations, or implications of the writing, there must be a story the reader can follow.

Stories Engage the Heart and the Mind

Often, our stories—even stories of the most detached among us—are, in the end, stories of the life of the human heart. Stories reflect the embodiment of our experiences and knowledge. Finding the heart's words may be just what your story needs (Pelias, 2004). Where are you, the researcher as human being, in this research? What are you feeling as you enter and inhabit the scene or as you go along or as you walk through something or walk away or move on? Stories also engage the mind of the author and the reader by pushing toward new interpretations of human experience. The goal of autoethnography is to affect both the heart and the mind.

Emotions and Memories Are Useful Data

Human experience is mysterious, in part, because of the (irrational, unpredictable, delightful, painful) emotional terrain we inhabit. This terrain is marked by our previous experiences; its contours are laid out over a lifetime of memories and emotional moments. And sometimes we just stumble into emotions or memories, like stumbling into a sudden rise or dip in the landscape, an unexpected turn in the road, or some rapids in the river of life. Many autoethnographic narratives are about this emotional terrain, along with events, encounters, and insights that change us (e.g., epiphanies). We are all familiar with the afflictions and delights of human emotion and the bumpy road of memory. Wrapped in the mysterious emotional moments of human life are the long histories—the stories and the memories—that serve as the filters through and with which we come to our present experience. Following the lead of emotion and memory, we piece together the meaning of our existence.

Stories Are Sites of Identification

For a story to compel us, readers have to identify in some way with what is going on in the story. We see ourselves somewhere in or near the story.

Readers feel the resonance of a good story in their hearts and lives. Compelling stories resonate with us because they reflect some aspect(s) of ourselves or our experiences. They speak to our desires or aspirations because they invoke our challenges and troubles, or they ring true or seem familiar. Sometimes they do all these things and touch on all points in between. For example, many of us have felt that mysterious feeling we call "love," but it often takes a story to evoke or remind us of its hold on us, its trials and tribulations, its joys and sorrows. Human identification with the heart stories of other humans is how stories move us to action. Identification is at the heart of the author's relationship with readers.

Stories Are Transformative

Striking stories work on the consciousness of the writer and the reader; they change us. As an aspiring (or seasoned) autoethnographer, you walked into a predicament: You chose to do autoethnographic research, a tough row to hoe. And now, assuming you want others to care about your research, you want to craft a compelling story. You want to do this because you want to transform the world, if only in a small way, even if it means moving only one person. Not many people aspire to do even that. Those of us who do are often in a bind, caught up in the mystery of it all, feeling our way through this mysterious terrain. Fortunately (or perhaps, unfortunately), sometimes, there is only one way out. You must write your way through the mystery. And you will be transformed.

GETTING STARTED

Given that we humans are *homo narrans* (Fisher, 1985)—the storytelling and story-consuming creature—this story-gift, regardless of form, seems to be ample reason to do autoethnographic work. Furthermore, autoethnography comes from the insight that, although life is a performance, as noted earlier, much of it is improvisational. To be an autoethnographer requires a willingness to surrender to the creative process and the spontaneous and imaginative memory-infused life of the writer as social commentator. Autoethnographers embrace the power of imagination and improvisation, while connecting to and engaging structure, history, and tradition (Poulos, 2019). Autoethnography is a form of *social and communicative praxis* (coming to know through action, making sense through communication) that proceeds more like jazz music (improvising within structure) rather than classical music (set rules and regulations). Jazz musicians talk about this improvisational impulse as a kind of loosely coordinated "flow" or "jamming" (Eisenberg, 1990). What follows are some specific guidelines you can use to cultivate and begin your auto-ethnographic writing practice: (a) Engage the flow of writing, (b) develop disciplined writing habits, and (c) strive to write evocatively.

Today, I want the words to take me where they want. I want to follow along, see where this writing goes, ride the wave of words to an unknown destination. All I have to start with is an image. This is not unprecedented, of course. When William Faulkner (1929/1990) was asked where he got the idea for *The Sound and the Fury*, he reportedly said, "A muddy little girl climbed down out of a tree" (Moreland, 2007). A single image started a sprawling 326-page novel. Those of you who have read the book know that it's not about a muddy little girl climbing down out of a tree. It's about the Compson family and their struggles, and it is written largely in stream of consciousness. That one shimmering image—the muddy little girl—started the flow of a great stream, a stream of writing that has become known as one of the great novels in U.S. history. My image is much more literal and directly related to how I see the writing process today—or, at least, its opening moments. It is me, flying into a big river—an image that came to me in a dream last night. The dream began with a specific memory, one I had not called up in years.

When I was a young man, I trained to be a river rafting guide in the mountains of Colorado. We trained on none other than the Colorado River. Before our first ride through Class 5 rapids, we were instructed on what to do if we fell out of the boat. "You can't fight the current," our instructor said. "If you try, you'll likely drown. What you do is really quite simple. Place your hands under your butt to protect it from rocks. Lean back and point your feet downstream. Eventually, you'll make your way toward one shore or the other by pointing your feet diagonally toward the closest one. And the current will carry you over. . . . You have to sense the river, feel its flow. When you feel you're in part of the current that might help you aim for shore, whether immediately after you fall in or half a mile downstream, point your feet toward the shore. If you make it into an eddy, you're golden. Just get out of the water when you can and wait for us. We'll pick you up." Are these concrete, specific instructions? Maybe. But I couldn't help thinking I had just heard an extended metaphor.

We were in paddle boats (with no oars), which require teamwork, everyone paddling like mad to get us through the rapids alive. I liked the front position. I liked being in the action. Sure enough, as soon as we hit the big rapids, the boat buckled, and I felt myself flying through the air. I think I must have shot about 10 feet straight up, and the boat ran right under me. That first shock when I hit the water, which was recently melted snow runoff (it was early June) at this 9,000-foot altitude, got my attention. And before I knew it, the river was taking me where it wanted to. I just leaned back and pointed my feet. What else could I do? The power of that current was awe-inspiring.

That's what I want to do with this writing today. I have been planning everything these last 8 years. After 8 years as chair of my department, I am tired. Tired of politics, tired of dealing with all the problems, tired of managing, tired of planning every move. I have been forced to follow protocols and systems and procedures and policies. Having just stepped down at the end of my second 4-year term, I feel like I have been let out of prison. And I want to be free, to dance in the sunlight, to play, to not follow the rules, to not formulate a 5-year plan.

Today, I just want to slip into the river (of writing) and see where the (autoethnographic) current takes me. In my dream, I came to understand that I was writing, that I was the author of this story but that the writing itself had gotten away from me. I had set out to write a tale about how we might write our way toward understanding, sharing a deeper meaning, coming to grips with what it means to be a human being in this troubled and fractured world, healing trauma and loss and grief, gaining richer emotional resonance, more fully following the contours of memory and experience, fully participating in community, interpreting culture, evoking embodied experience in this human lifeworld, and engaging in intensive reflection and reflexivity. But I had fallen into the stream, and the flow was having its way with me.

As I said, though, in my dream, I gradually became aware that I was the author of this stream of writing, but the writing seemed to lack direction. I probably should have been more structured in my writing approach, I found myself thinking. And maybe I should cool it with the spicy food before bed. But then, I quickly thought, Maybe it's not too late. Maybe I can just start right here, rewriting the story, taking it from the brink of disaster to something new, a breakthrough, a moment, a turning point. And as I wrote, I found myself taken by the flow of the words and carried into a new place, a place where writing itself is a mysterious and powerful and open-ended process where, like Forrest Gump's box of chocolates, you never know what you're gonna get (Zemeckis, 1994), and this—this right here—is what you got.

So what? I have now written three pages of experimental text based on a single image or metaphor that may or may not prove fruitful in serving my mission of helping the reader learn how this organic process of writing autoethnography works. So, let me just state the punch line: Three pages is more than zero pages, and these three illuminate the practice of flow. The point is to open up the flow of the writing. The point is to sit down and write without worrying about any rules, restrictions, or even goals and see where the writing takes you. Like running the river, you let yourself "go with the flow" to see where it may (or may not) lead. I may mine a single sentence out of this text for future use. And I may not. Maybe it just got me writing. Far too many writers complain about "writer's block," about staring for hours at a blank screen. Writing in a stream (or river) of consciousness is one way to ride right through that obstacle.

And that is how the flow of autoethnography works, at least at the outset. It is about writing your way through experience to gain a deeper understanding of the flow of events, memories, encounters, or objects in your world. It is about making your way through the rapids and the eddies and all the spaces in between. It is about coming to grips with a way of doing research that deeply involves the researcher-as-author in a studied practice of attunement, absorption, participation, observation, and writing. It is about writing and writing and writing some more, then editing, rewriting, and writing some more.

Once you have chosen autoethnographic writing as a way of life, you will find yourself embracing the notion that just about anything can serve to prompt the writing process. I began this section about flow with an image from memory that emerged in a dream—me, flying out of a raft and into a river. From that particular image's arrival, I tried to create this story of how to proceed as a writer of autoethnography. What image, event, or artifact might trigger the autoethnographic ride down the river is not always predictable. Over the past 20 years, I have written autoethnographic stories prompted by a photograph, a car accident, a song lyric, a shattered drinking glass, a big explosive moment in our culture, a classroom argument, a fragment of a memory, a conversation, the death of a loved one, a whispered secret, a big event, a small event, a film, a cultural phenomenon, a business meeting, a chance encounter, an insult, a conflict, 9/11, the birth of a child, an empty nest, an illness, an innuendo, an interruption, a classroom dialogue, the rogue acts of a bad leader, a dog fight, a relationship gone sour, a relationship starting to heal, a kid getting run over by a car, a relationship beginning, an anthrax scare, a mature relationship, a fascinating dialogue, falling in love, a friendship, a lost friendship, a weird family dynamic, a lie, a difficult truth, an addiction, suicidal thoughts, a wounded institution, a wounded community, a tenure fight, a wounded person, a note of joy, an academic conference, just playing around, an artifact or simple everyday object, and more. I have thought long and hard and often about how this kind of writing works:

> For some time I have been contemplating the idea that the process of writing the so-called new ethnography (Goodall, 2000) just comes on me, carries me along, throws me down, pulls me up short, pushes me, cajoles me, and catches me up in a wave of action, passion, and rising spirit. The writing *carries me*, not the other way around. I fall into it, and it takes me where it wants. Sometimes the ride is fast and exciting, sometimes cool and refreshing, sometimes overwhelming and scary, sometimes incredibly invigorating, always fascinating. (Poulos, 2019, p. 46)

I can't tell you exactly how to fall into the stream of writing. You have to take the plunge yourself and point your feet in the direction of the flow. My strongest advice is to start writing and then discipline yourself to continue writing.

BUILDING MOMENTUM

Once you have started the autoethnographic adventure, your next challenge will be to continue. You will have to work to build momentum here.

Develop Disciplined Writing Habits

The best writing habit you can cultivate is to write every day. Daily practice at anything is bound to make the practitioner better over time. To sustain the life of an autoethnographer, the writer must commit to writing habits as a part of daily research practice. The writing has to be good writing. And the best way to get good at something is to practice regularly. The autoethnographer, as a writer of life, must first and foremost attune him- or herself to the practice of using writing as a fitting response to life as it unfolds. And then, as Bud Goodall (2000, 2007), Carolyn Ellis (2004), and Anne Lamott (1995) have urged, you plant your butt in the seat and write. Every day. Or as many days as there are on the calendar. Or at least as many days as you possibly can. My practice is to write every morning before I do other work-like things. I brew my coffee, I sit, I begin. Sometimes what I write is golden. Sometimes, it leads nowhere. Often enough, there is something worthy that comes from this habit.

As I sit here now, writing this chapter, I am drawn to write about my father. At the same time, this particular call is a painful one. So, I must follow the disciplined habit of writing into and through that pain. You see, my dad died exactly 1 month ago today. The loss hangs heavy in the background of my day-to-day life. Today, it has risen to the surface. And I fall back in memory to a time when my dad was, for lack of a better word, my superhero. When I was 4 years old, Dad decided to enter seminary at the University of the South in Sewanee, Tennessee. For 3 years, we lived in a mountaintop paradise— a densely wooded 13,000-acre college campus. It was an idyllic setting and a beautiful place for a childhood to unfold. It was the mid-1960s, and I ran free and wild through the forest as a little boy should.

My most vivid memory from that time was on a Saturday morning sometime in the middle of autumn. We walked the long, winding path to the Sewanee Tigers football field to watch a game. I don't remember much about the football, but I do remember feeling special. I couldn't see, so my dad lifted me up, and put me atop a stone pillar above the crowd. He handed me a pom-pom on a stick, and I remember waving it wildly as the fans cheered. I also remember wondering, briefly, why these tigers were purple and white when all the other tigers I had seen were yellow and black. But mostly, I just loved being there with my dad.

On the way home, I was tired. I couldn't make the long journey under my own power. So, Dad lifted me up again, and I rode home happily on his shoulders. That is the last clear memory I have of my dad spending time with me, paying full attention to me, and just letting me be a little kid. After that, he got caught up in his studies and work. As life progressed, Dad became distant. He only seemed to surface to enact discipline—mostly, when I was acting like a child or, when I became an adult, for acting like an independent adult.

Much of our time together—which became rarer and rarer as the years unfolded and my options opened up—was spent in a battle of wills. He was of the opinion that I should eat my black-eyed peas because he said I should. I was of the opinion that I would rather eat dog food. So, I sat at the kitchen table, refusing to eat my peas or my lima beans, and he tried to force me to eat them. I was not allowed to leave the table until they were gone. So, naturally, I fed them to the dog, one at a time, surreptitiously.

Later, he was of the opinion that I should agree with all his opinions, no matter how outlandish. I was of a different mind. So, as the years progressed, the distance between my father and I grew into a chasm. Some of this distance seemed to be attributable to his depression, which appeared to be triggered by the deaths of his brother, sister, and father in rapid succession over 18 months or so, starting when I was about 12. Some of it seemed to flow from his tendency toward living a workaholic life (in which he was absorbed most of every day of the week), and some of it was just that he was a difficult person to get along with. Irascible Greek men often are, at least in my experience. Although I admit I had my own streak of defiance and perhaps even defensiveness as a boy and young man, the truth is my father never showed much of an interest in developing a close relationship with me. So, for many years, we did not have one.

Late in his life (sometime during the past 5 years or so), it all came to a head. As a result of a conflict over a long-held resentment against something I did as a young preteenager, I took him to see my psychotherapist. And the healing process began. I came to realize that my dad was suffering, and as he began telling me stories of his life, I came to understand why. His father was largely absent and treated him harshly when he was present. His mother was controlling and nearly smothered his personhood until he broke free to go to college. My dad simply passed along this legacy. But he paid a price. His depression eventually worked its way into physical symptoms that included chronic pain at a level most people would be unable to tolerate. By the end of his life, his body was failing him so badly—he was wracked with congestive heart failure, chronic obstructive pulmonary disease, rheumatoid arthritis, spinal stenosis, and some unnamed neurological disorder that caused a near-constant tremor throughout his body—that he was unable to muster the strength to go on. His reserves were exhausted. He was dying.

Those last 8 weeks, which he spent mostly in and out of a hospital and rehab center, were grueling. I know he was suffering greatly. Finally, in early July 2019, we brought him home and admitted him to hospice care. He died within 36 hours. His suffering was over. But the family's is not. This is a new and different kind of grief. When you lose a parent, it is an experience that only those who have been down this road can understand. The ground shifts under your feet. The center did not hold (Yeats, 1919/1996).

As an autoethnographer who studies trauma and loss and grief and associated emotions, I have written much about grief in these past few years. Loss, and the grief that accompanies it, is one of the most difficult trials of human life. People often have a hard time of it. My family is no exception.

Several years ago, seven people in my close circle of family and friends passed away over about 11 months. There were days during those long months when I thought the grief would sink me deep into despair and leave me there, wrung out, incapable of going on. But during this time, I was engaging a daily practice of writing my way through the grief (Poulos, 2012c, 2014). Toward the end of that period, I wrote, "Writing my way through the grief I feel has offered me something I knew I was searching for all along. It has offered me the remedy for despair" (Poulos, 2014, p. 358). I was not wrong. The writing seemed to work on me as a kind of *therapeutikos* (Greek for "ministering, healing, cleansing"). As I write today (November 2019), another five people in my close circle have died, this time over about 4 months. I am still writing my way through the grief.

Strive to Write Evocatively

The clearest call of autoethnography is to write about experience evocatively, with richness, imagery, clarity, emotional texture, and depth. Evocative writing is a way of constructing written research texts that conjure, arouse, or elicit vivid images, deep meanings, or intense emotions. Evocative autoethnographic writing is explored via an intensive search through these layers of imagery, meaning, and emotion. An example may help to illustrate what evocative autoethnography looks like.

One day, in the middle of grieving my dad's passing, I find myself at my mom and dad's house, helping my mom look for the original copy of his will.

We are searching through a pile of boxes filled to the brim with various papers, from bank statements to old receipts to miscellaneous forms, statements, and bills of every sort. There are grocery receipts from 1990. We even stumble upon checks and bank statements from the 1970s. The man kept everything (except, apparently, his will). As I search, I happen to look up at his bookshelf. It is piled high with miscellaneous boxes, baskets, books, and other assorted objects. And for some reason, I notice a baseball, perched precariously on a stack of books. "Now that's odd," I find myself thinking.

Sure, a baseball is an ordinary object. There is normally nothing remarkable about seeing a baseball, except that my father didn't play baseball. Besides, it doesn't fit where it's sitting, and in any event, my father had not touched a baseball in decades, as far as I know. He had not even played catch in over 48 years. I know this detail because I would have been the one to play catch with him. I am the only baseball player in this family. When I was a kid, I was a baseball fanatic. I was obsessed. After my early years of wanting to be a cowboy, a pirate, a cowboy-pirate, an astronaut, a space-pirate-cowboy, and a spy, and once I grew out of those impossible early childhood fantasies and had developed some physical coordination, I seriously wanted to grow up to be a baseball player. For years, when adults asked me what I wanted to be when I grew up, my answer never changed: "I want to play baseball." Indeed, when I found out that people get paid money to do my favorite thing on earth, I was on a mission! I started playing little league baseball as soon as they would let me. At the time, I was about age 6.

I practiced and played every chance I got. Over the years, I developed solid skills as a fielder. I could catch a baseball! My hand–eye coordination was excellent, my reflexes were quick, and my throwing arm was accurate and strong. I could play any position. Indeed, I did play every position at one point or another. But my favorites—my usual spots—were shortstop and second base. My hitting was only average; it definitely needed work. But my fielding was on point; I could snag a line drive or a hard grounder, and I was pretty good at turning a double play. And I played and played and played. I played all the way through high school.

But my dad did not engage with my obsession. In fact, he rarely even played a simple game of catch with me. He liked to watch baseball on TV, but he almost never played catch with me, and he never came to my games. He was always working. Or watching TV. So, why would he have a baseball sitting on his bookshelf so many years later, decades after I hung up my glove to pursue other things?

I walk over and pick it up. I immediately realize that this is not just any baseball. It's a very specific ball. I examine it closely. It's a little league–size ball made by Spalding. And the ball has signatures on it, now a little faded after so many years: Chuck Robinson, Steve Miller, John Crawford, David Pulliam, Chris Poulos, Ted Harris, Lonnie Morrow, David McMullin. Some smart aleck even signed it "Babe Ruth," and another wrote "X." As I read the names, I realize who these people are. They are the 1971 Twins, one of the better teams on which I had played. This was the year—the one year—when my dad started showing up to my baseball games. Quite suddenly, after all those years of no-shows, my dad decided to be the assistant coach of my little league team. So, this is not just any baseball. It is a significant baseball. This baseball is a sign.

To unpack the meaning of this particular baseball showing up right now at this moment, in this way, just after my dad's death, I have to go back to a conflict that erupted about 5 years ago. This conflict was a rerun of an earlier conflict my dad and I had about 20 years ago, which in turn was a rerun of a conflict we had nearly 50 years ago. Indeed, it is a version of the conflict I mentioned earlier, involving the black-eyed peas, which began occurring with regularity some 56 years ago, though this one is specifically about baseball. Or so it might seem.

As I gaze at the ball in my hand, it occurs to me now that my dad and I had a lot of conflict reruns throughout his life. My dad, who spent much of his life planted in front of the television, knew a fair amount about reruns. Let's just say he exceeded the national average of television viewing. The TV was always on. Most of his favorite shows were old reruns from the 1960s and 1970s—shows he had watched when they were first on TV and many times since. So, I suppose having reruns of events in his everyday life was not too much of a stretch.

It is also important to note that my dad had a notoriously thin skin. Stories of dad getting mad at a store clerk, a customer service representative, a waiter, or an insurance agent are common, legendary even. And his usual tactic is to shun those people once he gets mad. Nobody can disown you more thoroughly than an irascible Greek. But he holds on to the resentments and nurses them. When the subject of the resentment is mentioned, his feelings are raw—as if the transgression just took place, even if many years have passed since the triggering incident. This rerun is particularly intense. It is a conflict about power. And resentment. And mostly, it is a conflict about being a father and a son and our proper places in the pecking order.

Five years ago, I am sitting in my parents' living room. They are dog sitting my sister's Pekingese, Teddy. It is important to note that when I was a kid, I was the one with pets. I had dogs, cats, rabbits, gerbils, and fish. The only proviso was that I had to train, care for, and feed them all. I read everything I could get my hands on about raising animals. It is safe to say I developed some real expertise in these matters at a young age. My parents mostly ignored my animals. When I grew up and left home, as soon as I could, I got a dog. And another. My wife (also a dog person) and I have always had two dogs. Now, 38 years into our relationship, we have had seven dogs. We have dog sat for at least a dozen others over the years. It is safe to say that, having attended obedience classes and private training sessions for many years now, I know a bit about dog training. My dad knows absolutely nothing. I tell you all this because the dog is what triggered the conflict. Or so it seemed at the time. In this scene, my mom is trying to get Teddy to come to her.

MOM: Teddy, come! [*No response.*]

MOM: Teddy, come! [*Again, no response.*]

MOM: [*Louder*] TEDDY, COME!

ME: Does he know that word?

DAD: [*Sharply*] What did you say?

ME: Has anyone taught him what "come" means?

DAD: He should just come when you tell him to. Stupid dog.

ME: He's not stupid. Dogs don't know English. You have to teach it to them.

DAD: [*Furious and red-faced now*] I know all about dogs! That dog is stupid! You don't know what you're talking about!

ME: [*Thinking that his fury came quickly*] I know a thing or two about dogs, Dad. [*I know this is a mistake. He has lost his grip. But I wade in anyway.*] I've raised and trained a LOT of dogs in my life.

DAD: [*Stands, in a rage, shouting*] YOU LISTEN TO ME! I KNOW MORE ABOUT DOGS THAN YOU DO. AND YOU DON'T TALK TO ME LIKE THAT! I KNOW ABOUT DOGS!

ME: Dad. Why are you so angry right now?

DAD: I'M NOT ANGRY! YOU'RE DISRESPECTFUL!

ME: What do you mean?

DAD: YOU'VE NEVER LISTENED TO A WORD I SAY!

ME: [*I do not think I was being disrespectful here, but I breathe, trying to get him to dial it down a notch, then pause a bit longer before I reply.*] Tell me what you're talking about, please.

DAD: [*Still red faced*] EVER SINCE THAT YEAR, I WAS YOUR BASEBALL COACH.

ME: [*Thinking that this came out of left field*] You mean when I was 12?

DAD: Yes. That sounds about right. I was your coach, remember?

ME: Yes, vaguely. It's been a while. Let's see—about 44 years or so.

DAD: WELL, YOU WOULDN'T LISTEN TO ME!

ME: About what? I honestly don't remember.

DAD: I TRIED TO COACH YOU. I TRIED TO HELP YOU HIT BETTER! I COULD SEE WHAT YOU WERE DOING WRONG. BUT YOU WOULDN'T LISTEN. YOU IGNORED ME.

ME: Right. Sorry about that. I was 12. Twelve-year-old boys are insufferable. And besides, that was the first time you'd ever even watched me play baseball. How was I to know you knew what you were doing? I'd never seen you hit a baseball. So maybe I had a chip on my shoulder. Maybe I had no idea why you were suddenly trying to teach me to play baseball, after so many years of not showing up. Again, I was 12. All 12-year-old boys are like that. But why are you still so mad?

DAD: YOU'RE SO DAMN DISRESPECTFUL!

ME: I'm disrespectful? You insult me every single time I see you. And you yell—a lot.

DAD: GET OUT!

ME: [*Walking out the door*] Okay, I have to go.

After that encounter, I invite my dad to come to a joint session with me and my psychotherapist. In fact, I insist on it. Clearly, we have issues. As we begin talking about the incident that precipitated this meeting, my dad quickly gets angry again. His face turns red as he tells the therapist about what I have come to call "the baseball incident." He starts pointing his finger and jabbing it at my face. He is blistering mad.

THERAPIST: What's the finger for?

DAD: What?

THERAPIST: You can put your finger down. You won't be needing it. Try to relax and just tell the story.

DAD: [*For some reason, disarmed by this, he takes a breath.*] Fair enough.

As I listen to him tell my therapist about how he tried to coach me, tried to show me, tried to help me, I realize I must have hurt his feelings then. I should note here that I do not remember any of what he is talking about. I remember playing ball that year. I played ball every year. I vaguely remember him being at my games, standing by the dugout. I have no recollection of him trying to coach me. I certainly don't remember refusing his advice. And I carry no ill will about it at all. But it is as fresh for him as if it happened yesterday. And he's still furious about it, 44 years later.

As we continue, he tells the therapist that I have always been a rebel, that I never accepted his authority. "No shit," I find myself thinking. "I mean, black-eyed peas, for God's sake." I feel compassion for him, realizing he is wounded. For him, my refusal to listen was traumatic. But I also know that I will not—cannot—just let him continue wounding me in retaliation. I also realize that my dad has a lot at stake here. He is trying to save face. And he simply cannot accept that I don't just automatically surrender to his authority. I feel compassion, but given how long this battle has been raging, I also feel compelled to take constructive action. Because in addition to flying off the handle about this or about snakes (Poulos, 2012b) or about just about anything that comes up, he has gotten into that bad habit of insulting me every time I see him. He usually makes some crack about my weight, something I am self-conscious about and have struggled mightily with over the years. He knows his insults hurt me. That is why he does it. He is trying to establish dominance. I have asked him to stop. He continues anyway.

When it is my turn, I say, "Dad, you know I'm not 12 now, right? I am very sorry I hurt you when I was 12, but that was a VERY LONG TIME AGO. It's been 44 years. I'm 56 years old. If I haven't surrendered yet, I'm not likely to. I don't know why you could never let me just be who I am, but now you don't really have a choice in the matter. You're my father, and I love you, but I've been a grown man for many years now. Hell, I've raised my own kids to adulthood. Now, here's how it plays out from here on. You can stop insulting me, and you can stop demanding that I agree with everything you say, and you can stop shouting at me at the slightest provocation, or we can end this relationship right here, right now. I'm setting a hard boundary here. No more insults. No more shouting. No more bullshit. I don't need this, and I don't need you." Dad looks stunned. A single tear streams down his cheek. This rebuke of my dad may sound harsh, but he needed that boundary. It occurs to me that nobody has ever told him that there are boundaries you just cannot cross. For many years, he has been poking, prodding, and attacking me. He had to be set straight. I read his tear as a tear of regret. I have one of my own, in fact.

Interpret Your Experience

That day is a turning point. At his request, we decide to perform a ritual purging of our resentments. We agree to write them all down on paper, then go into his backyard and burn them, casting the ashes to the wind. So, we do just that. After that, things ease up between my dad and me. He starts to tell me stories of his life. And for the first time in my life, I find myself listening to him, which, it turns out, is what he wanted all along.

Over the next 5 years, until his death, our relationship begins to heal. And the stories flow. There are a couple of minor altercations, but nothing with such intensity. Eventually, we both learn to let go a little. I am fully aware that he is not the father of my dreams, nor am I the son he always wanted. But we are who we are. And yet, we managed to reach a kind of peace together.

Then one day, my dad died (July 5, 2019). And the grief just washed over me. I found myself trembling uncontrollably, as if I had taken on his neurological disorder. It hit me like a ton of bricks: My world had fundamentally changed forever. And the tears flowed. I found myself sunken to the floor, sobbing. Today, I miss my dad. I wish I could hug him.

Now, back to that baseball. As I sit here now, it is perched on my writing desk, next to my computer. There is history in that ball. There is some pain stored beneath its skin. But there are also some good memories. As I recall, we won a lot of games that year and came in first place. I played on the league's all-star team that summer. I like to think my dad helped with that, even if I did not want to admit he was helping me.

Still, today, I cannot help wondering: Why did that baseball show up again? Why now? And I cannot help thinking: Because I needed to write this story, I needed to heal a little bit more.

I have written autoethnographic texts about my relationship with my father over the years (Poulos, 2012a, 2012b, 2019). And I have written about how this relationship is a doorway to understanding a whole generation of relationships between boys and their fathers. My dad was born in 1934; I was born in 1958. As the baby boom burst forth, from about 1944–1964, large-scale societal change came and disrupted the status quo, especially in the years following World War II. And as the 1960s came into view, social upheaval (civil rights, the women's movement, the anti-war movement, rock 'n' roll music) truly shifted the ground under father–son relationships. A generation whose rallying cry was "question authority" no longer stood still while fathers issued edicts. Authoritarianism, which had failed miserably in World War II, was not going to fly. We were rebels, and we started at a young age. Fathers who had kids when they were relatively young, as my dad did in his early 20s, were ill-prepared for what was to come. They had been taught to demand submission. But what they got was outright rebellion. Now there is a good deal of evidence that a whole generation of sons experienced difficult—sometimes even broken—relationships with their fathers (Keen, 1992; Osherson, 2001).

And this story speaks into that father–son rift in a very personal way. For my purposes here, it serves as a clear example of the birth of an autoethnographic story that had to be written. And like Faulkner's muddy little girl, a single object (that significant baseball) opened up the story—a story that is only nominally about baseball. "The baseball incident" is, after all, "the father–son breakthrough." And that is how autoethnography works. It grows out of an urge, an impulse, a need, a spark—or a loss, a feeling, a memory, an artifact, a trauma—that leads to a story that needs to be written.

4 PROCESS AND CRAFT

In this chapter, I explore how the writing of autoethnography proceeds from the assumptions and practices outlined previously and how various kinds of autoethnographic texts may be structured. The "baseball incident" story is a pretty straightforward narrative—with an embedded flashback—about a series of events triggered by the death of my father and the subsequent sighting of an object. As you can see, the narrative moves through a series of possibilities that might help to make sense of the object that seemed to present itself to me.

In my previous work, I have called this sort of stumbling onto an object—or an encounter, an event, an obstacle, or a revelation, seemingly at random—*accidental autoethnography* (Poulos, 2008b, 2012a, 2012b, 2019). It is accidental in the sense that it is not something the autoethnographer was necessarily seeking, at least not directly. It is something you stumble onto. Indeed, as we make our way through everyday life, we often stumble into opportunities. Of course, to make more of it than a small passing event, the accidental autoethnographer must pay attention and make something of its emergence into consciousness in and through writing about it.

https://doi.org/10.1037/0000222-004
Essentials of Autoethnography, by C. N. Poulos

The idea is that the accidental autoethnographer attunes him- or herself to the lifeworld, looking for signs that something meaningful might be afoot. Sometimes these signs are what Goodall (1996) called "divine signs"—objects, symbols, or events that draw the autoethnographer into the mystery of being and whose reading may lead to a transcendent experience. In this case, the baseball carries something of the divine in its wake. Stumbling on this baseball as I searched for my father's last will and testament led to a story about an ongoing conflict between my dad and me (description, evocation), which led to a rumination on this particular relationship (connection), which then turned into an attempt at making sense of this particular father–son relationship in the context of father–son relationships of men of my generation (analysis and cultural critique). From this point, given the space to do it, I could work through the larger implications of wounded father–son relationships for family communication systems and practices. Indeed, I have done just that in my previous work (Poulos, 2012a, 2012b, 2019). Here, I turn to other matters.

Indeed, this last turn in the road leads to a deeper reflection on my grief. Naturally, it could have turned in another direction. It could have gone otherwise. But it took me right down into my deep, deep sadness at my father's passing—sadness about how things were, about how things could have been, about the final shattering of our together-lives, and about the raw fact that, despite the difficulties we experienced in our relationship, I will miss him every day for the rest of my life. But I wrote it to demonstrate how a single moment in time (noticing the baseball) could trigger the crafting of a meaning-making narrative autoethnographic text. I now turn to a more direct discussion of the writing process of an (accidental or otherwise) autoethnographer.

A major premise of the autoethnographic movement in qualitative inquiry is that we should attend closely to the craft of evocative writing because we use writing as our primary method of qualitative inquiry. How we say what we say matters. Words—their arrangements, tones, rhythms, patterns, and connections to each other and the reader—matter. A lot. So, first and foremost, the autoethnographer strives to write a striking, evocative, compelling tale of the field (Ellis, 2004; Goodall, 2000; Van Maanen, 1988). Autoethnographic writing is a way of constructing research texts that conjure, arouse, or elicit vivid images, deep meanings, and intense emotions. Autoethnographic writing requires an intensive search through these layers of imagery, meaning, and emotion. Autoethnographic writing—writing that "shows forth" or brings forward into the present text an amalgam of images, meanings, and emotions—speaks to the heart of the reader. Autoethnographic writing is rich, textured, and moving.

For example, in her writing about her experience as a sexual abuse survivor, Rambo (2013) explored what happened as she recovered her memories in her therapist's office and likened it to drowning: "Flailing, I crash through the bottom of the boat. As I sink backwards into the silent depths, for a split second, I see everything as beautiful. Then I panic at the falling debris and breathe water into my lungs" (p. 628). Here, she evoked the sense of drowning in the terror of what was happening to her as she remembered what her father did to her when she was a small child. She continued, this time choking, gasping for air:

> As I thrash about. . . . It happens, over and over again; in my therapist's office, at home in bed, or on the living room floor. I am choking, my throat shut, my shoulders pinned to the ground, this is happening "to" me. (p. 631)

In the end, she crafted a narrative about living with and through symptoms of posttraumatic stress disorder (PTSD) caused by repeated sexual abuse in childhood. Autoethnographic writing calls powerful images into the reader's consciousness. These are multidimensional images. Rambo is drowning, she is choking, she is suffocating . . . and in everyday life, she finds herself twitching. Autoethnographic writing evokes images of how things are or were—of people, places, events, memories, traumas, and emotions.

These images are integral to scenes, which the writing is about and through which the power of the writing is accomplished. And these scenes show a sense of place (of being somewhere) and a sense of time (of being there when). So, autoethnographic writing shows forth images or scenes imbued with place and time and action. Autoethnographic writing expresses, invokes, provokes, and evokes deep, painful, joyous feelings and everything in between. Autoethnography connects writer and reader experientially, spatially, temporally, mentally, and spiritually—through imagery, meaning, and emotion. Good autoethnography is so vivid it carries you into the writer's world, brings you to heights, drops you to lows, shines a light, brings a shadow, pulls you into agony, sweeps you into joy, breaks your heart, makes you hurt, gnaws at you, makes you twitch. You see images in your mind's eye, feel your place in the story, identify with the author, know deeper meanings you've been hoping to grasp, and feel the pain, sadness, anger, outrage, joy, hope, and ecstasy of life.

In this scene, I show how my father's legendary temper shook and shaped and transformed me:

> The door slams, too hard, shaking the whole car. My door is yanked open, and with a quick jerk, I find myself on the side of the road. He drags me around to the back of the car, says, "Bend over and grab your ankles." I hesitate. But the glare I get tells me I'd better comply. Slowly, I bend forward, grab my ankles. His belt slides through the loops fluidly, snaps as he doubles it. I clench my teeth

and bite my lip as the blows rain down . . . but I will not break, will not cry, will not let the pain win. And I will not let him know he is getting to me. I will not. (Poulos, 2012a, p. 325)

Autoethnographic writing requires the author to attend carefully to the construction of the text. This construction process requires a strong sense of the importance of word craft. So, most autoethnographers write, rewrite, edit, write some more, edit some more, rewrite even more. To put it bluntly, all good writing is the product of rewriting. Unlike some of our students, we don't turn in our "shitty first drafts" (Lamott, 1995, p. 20). We use our words to craft images, emotions, signs, meanings, and vivid scenes into being, and we work on them, work with them, and write, edit, and rewrite.

CONSIDERATIONS

As noted earlier, sometimes you just start writing. And sometimes you have to consider some important features of the writing-as-inquiry process first. The following are some of the aspects of the writing-as-inquiry process that may need your attention.

- *Approach.* How do you approach the task of writing? How does writing fit into your scheme of conducting research? For the autoethnographer, the writing is the most important activity. Sure, you do your data gathering (poking around the neighborhood) work; that is, after all, a centerpiece of the ethnographic way of life. You're always doing it. But it bears repeating: Autoethnography is not "writing up" findings after the research is conducted. The research is ongoing, so the writing is ongoing. How will you make your way through this journey? What does your writing process look like, feel like, have you doing?

- *Purpose.* What goals, intentions, or possibilities are you questing after? What is your entry into qualitative inquiry for? What and whom does it serve, and how? Why on earth would you want to undertake such an arduous journey? Most autoethnographers write to transform something deeply personal or communal—suffering, memory, communication, family, points of view, interpretations, community, the heart of the reader, or something. What do you want your writing to do?

- *Form.* Where does your research story begin? Where does it end? How can you use beginnings and endings to navigate the middle of your story? What is the relationship between a "set up" and a "pay off" in your writing? How will you make your way from beginning to end, with some sort of coherence or meaningful form? What will your story look like? How will you and your readers make sense of what you're doing?

- *Voice*. How can you establish your (transformative, powerful, resonant, heart-filled) authorial voice and stake out your credibility as a writer or researcher? Who is the person telling this story? Why should we believe you? What will you reveal to us about yourself that will show forth your ethos?

- *Mystery*. What puzzle(s) are you trying to resolve, question, explore, or clarify? What surprises have you stumbled into in your search and research? How will you embrace and unpack the mystery? What new questions are arising as you go along?

- *Impact*. What makes your research story compelling? How can you use good writing to advance your story line(s)? How will you evoke or provoke something that will count as a contribution to the human conversation? How can you help your readers to come on a journey with you, into your world, and thus come to know and respond to the who, what, why, where, when, and how of your story? What will you do to draw the reader into your storied world?

Once you've pondered these queries (which you might want to consider pondering every day as a kind of writing road map or at least a faintly visible path), you can use them to guide you in your writing. You may not always know where you are going, but at least you will know a little bit about why you are going. In the following sections, I show how autoethnographers respond to the ongoing demands and conventions of this unique form of qualitative writing-as-inquiry.

NARRATIVE CONVENTIONS OF AUTOETHNOGRAPHY

In the simplest terms, a *story* can be defined as the showing forth of actions of significant characters along a stretch of time. The crafting of a good story is an art rather than a science, but as with any art form, it is useful to attend to some basic conventions. Good autoethnographers, in their quest to write a striking tale, often use many of the conventions of narrative fiction and creative non-fiction writing, adapted to the autoethnographic project, to animate their stories. The mantra of the autoethnographer is "show, don't tell." The demand to show the author's lifeworld to the reader leads the autoethnographer to work words into scenes, animated by the voice of the narrator, who offers up a world through thick description, action, dialogue, character development, various plot devices (e.g., flashbacks, temporal shifts, new obstacles), poetic or lyrical rhythms and melodies, vivid imagery, metaphor, simile, emotion, and so on. Autoethnographic texts can take many forms and structures, from lyrical essays to performance scripts to interactive dialogues to pieces that move back and forth across time, space, and everything in between. I discuss variations to this approach in the next chapter.

Meanwhile, it should be noted that the point of autoethnography, regardless of the form it may take, is to evoke a sense of what it is like to be in this lifeworld facing a particular memory, encounter, obstacle, conflict, observation, artifact, or sign and build a story to draw out or elicit a resonant response in the reader and to make sense, via analysis and interpretation of the story. The best autoethnographic writing is, therefore, not mere reporting on or writing up the results of completed research; rather, it is a studied and crafted attempt to draw a reader into a world and (one hopes) to move the reader to an engaged response (action, emotion, dialogue) as a result of reading a compelling story. Even if said action is simply feeling some genuine human emotion as a fitting response to the story, something important has occurred. In the end, autoethnographers strive to create texts that lead to personal, relational, and social transformation. These are stories with purpose.

Because how you tell a story with purpose matters, an autoethnographer pays a great deal of attention to how, when, and whether these recognizable story-crafting conventions are to be used. The basic idea is to write vivid, evocative scenes that help the reader feel as if he or she has entered the lifeworld inhabited by the writer. So, of course, the story must resonate with the reader in some profound way, even if the reader hasn't actually experienced the kinds of things the author is writing about.

For example, as noted earlier, Carol Rambo's story "Twitch" (in Jones et al., 2013) carries the reader into the storied world of a PTSD survivor so vividly that you might even feel yourself starting to twitch a bit. Indeed, as a reader of autoethnography, I have been drawn into many worlds, some familiar, some not so familiar. I have stood alongside a young Black girl growing up in rural North Carolina (Boylorn, 2012)—a life space as far from my White suburban upbringing as one can get, and yet, I was there. I have gone on the road with a wannabe rock star (Goodall, 1991), something I have only vaguely dreamed of, and yet, I was riding along with him. I have lived for a moment inside the world of war veterans trying to make sense of reentry into an ordinary world (Hunniecutt, 2018; Olt, 2018). I have walked through cancer treatment with a friend (Baglia, 2019). I have stood with a victim of sexual abuse (Fox, 1996), and I have mourned with a woman who wanted desperately to be a mother only to have nothing but miscarriages (Chester, 2003). None of these particular examples are drawn from (or even come close to) my experiences.

Indeed, some of these worlds are totally unfamiliar to me. And yet, I felt, as I read their stories, that I was with the authors. The worlds they open up are powerful doorways into a deeper understanding of our shared human condition. What all these works have in common is that the authors engage in writing that takes the reader into the "process of personally and academically reflecting on lived experiences that reveal the deep connection between the writer and her or his subject" (Goodall, 2000, p. 137).

Next, as you get truly serious about the craft of writing good autoethnography, you have to attend to several key conventions of narrative autoethnography (see Table 4.1).

Know Your Audience

What do I mean by "know your audience"? Ask yourself, Specifically, who are these people (my readers)? Who is the potential audience for your

TABLE 4.1. Conventions of Narrative Autoethnography

Convention	Questions or queries
1. Know your audience	Who are you writing for? What do your readers bring to the table?
2. Raise important questions and respond to them	What questions are you asking? Why do these questions matter? How will you respond?
3. Invite your readers into your world	How will you excite the curiosity of your reader?
4. Craft vivid scenes	How will you use thick description, and so forth, to build a sense of place and the passage of time?
5. Develop and deploy interesting characters	Who are the characters (including you) in your work? How will your reader get to know them?
6. Write compelling dialogue	Can you write vivid, natural, flowing dialogue to "flesh out" your characters?
7. Build a sense of action	How will you write actively and show characters doing things to bring your reader into the scene?
8. Attend to the passage of time	How will you show movement across time?
9. Evoke and invoke emotion	How will you help your readers feel with you?
10. Tie the story to theory	Can you connect the story to the theory or literature of your field?
11. Write some sort of coda (analysis or interpretation)	How will you interpret your story? What sort of analysis (however tentative) can you offer?
12. Write, edit, rewrite, and repeat	How will you continue to craft the writing to make it more compelling, vivid, evocative? Write. Edit. Rewrite. Repeat.

autoethnographic journal article or book? What do they care about? Of course, by far, the largest audience for autoethnographic work is other academics who do (or want to do) autoethnography or other forms of qualitative research. Whatever audience you can invite into your world—and persuade to stay—wants to read your good words. Make the most of that. In the end, your primary readership will be other academics—and their students—who are drawn to this kind of work. This is both good news and bad news. The good side is that these readers are predisposed (and trained) to read and get what they are looking for from this kind of work. The downside is that many of these people are trained in the method and are thus (potentially, at least) tough critics. So, the work has to be solid. And the writing has to be excellent. You should only be writing good stuff anyway. Besides, because you are now writing every day, honing your craft, you will likely become a better writer over time. But I recommend you ask yourself every single time you sit down to write: Who are my readers? How can I speak to their hearts and minds from my heart and mind? What motivates my readers to begin reading and to continue?

Some of the audience interest will be drawn strictly by subject matter, of course. Readers interested in trauma and loss, for example, are likely to search for and read articles on that subject. But don't think you can't ever reach people who aren't predisposed to be deeply interested in your subject. You have to hook those people. Indeed, you have to hook every reader somehow.

Raise Important Questions and Respond to Them

As noted earlier, the autoethnographer's quest is motivated by the mystery of being, which raises compelling questions. As autoethnographers, we ask important, moving, sometimes painful, and often insightful questions about the human condition. You have to make clear what your questions are, without hitting the reader over the head with them. As story drivers, the questions you ask are central, and as story elements, they are what moves the story to whatever ending you might find.

Invite Your Readers Into Your World

To invite readers into your world, you will have to find and use opening words that will draw your reader into the story and entice them to stay the course. The most important paragraph in your work may well be the first one. Some autoethnographers call this opening invitation "the hook" (Goodall, 2007). You are competing for the time of readers who are busy juggling other things.

You have to grab their attention right off the bat. That striking first sentence of that striking story you are writing will be the beginning of a relationship. Consider it carefully: How can I draw my readers into my world and keep their interest? As you craft your story, you will take your readers along with you. Consider this opening paragraph from H. L. Goodall, Jr.'s (1989) *Casing a Promised Land: The Autobiography of an Organizational Detective as Cultural Ethnographer*:

> You get out of the old school and move into the New South. You drive the U-Haul, wife and cat follow in the Renault. You turn off the interstate in lower Tennessee onto a two-lane blacktop that without mercy drops you into northern Alabama's cankerous lip. For the next thirty miles you glance eagerly into the rearview mirrors and see your wife's expression turn from hopeful optimism into a struggle for control over a basic instinct to flee. (p. 1)

I want to find out how this story goes. I want to know whether their life works out in that "cankerous lip" of northern Alabama. I want to know more about their ambivalence. And I want to know what they're going to do when they arrive at their new home. The opening excites the curiosity of the reader. The good opening raises compelling questions and opens the door to new ways of thinking and knowing. It raises a sense of mystery—a mystery worth pursuing. You want your reader to come along on a journey with you. To get that to happen, you have to issue a compelling invitation.

Craft Vivid Scenes

Writing vivid scenes that draw the reader into the lifeworld of the author requires studied attention to the details of everyday life and sentences crafted to build connections between the lifeworld of the author and that of the reader. As noted in Chapter 1, thick description—or vivid writing—is a method of observational and participatory writing that speaks to the senses, that offers rich detail about the surround (lifeworld) the researcher is submerged in. Autoethnographers use thick description to build a sense of place and the passage of time, attempting to pull the reader into the world shown forth in the story. For example,

> Take South Carolina #15 exit of I-85 heading up from Atlanta at the legal speed limit, pause at the stop sign at the end of the exit ramp, and—if you are prone to consider the meaning of such things—you see that you are now at a complex intersection of American culture . . . to the right, toward Anderson, are familiar signs of God-fearing, gun-toting interstate existence. Here are the popular corporate icons to fast self-service gas to which are not attached two-color convenience stores specializing in the sale of sugar-coated, high-calorie nothings displayed seductively in brightly colored plastic wrap. (Goodall, 1996, p. 27)

I can see this spot. I have been to this spot—well, not exactly this spot—but countless spots like it on numerous U.S. interstates. The thick description here evokes a vivid sense of place.

Develop and Deploy Interesting Characters

The main character in any autoethnography is the author. Most autoethnography is written in the first person, from the narrator's point of view. As the author, you have to build in your readers some sort of identification with your quest or plight. The reader connects with the author through the author's exposure of his or her inner, vulnerable self. Readers of autoethnography want to know who you are, how you feel, what you think about, what your personality is like, what your predilections and tastes are, and so on—they want to see themselves in you or at least imagine a connection.

As for other characters, the task is similar. You should introduce your readers to your characters as fully and richly as possible. Much of this can be accomplished via description and dialogue. The following is a brief description I wrote several years ago in my field notes for a piece on my grandfather's death.

> For some reason, when I think of him, I always think of his hands. When I was a little kid, I was fascinated by his hands. For some reason, they seemed really big to me, but that wasn't the most remarkable thing. His hands were hard, brown, tough, strong. I honestly thought that, while everyone else's hands were covered in skin, his were made of boot leather.
>
> My grandfather, James Norman Leckie, Sr., was strong, tough, independent, smart, restless. He was that guy who never really settled on a single career in a time when everyone else did. So he had six. He was a forester, a caretaker, a professor, an extension agent, a baker, a farmer, and probably some other things he didn't care to mention. But what always struck me about this powerful, sturdy man—he was about 5'7" tall, stocky, with strong leathery hands and piercing blue eyes and a shock of short-cropped but thick dark hair—was his confidence.

Now you know him a little, and you can picture him a bit.

Write Compelling Dialogue

Autoethnographers sometimes use dialogue between characters to advance the story. But the use of dialogue in a story should be natural, not contrived. Writing good dialogue into a story is perhaps the most difficult thing to pull off in autoethnographic writing. So, I caution writers to use it sparingly and with purpose.

Yet, as Ann Lamott (1995) pointed out, a single line of well-crafted dialogue can reveal more about a character and more about the purpose of the story than pages and pages of description. The writer has to be attuned to the rhythms and nuances of everyday conversation to pull it off. Listening becomes your primary observation tool. You have to listen to and understand how people talk in everyday life. Rendering natural-sounding conversation on the page requires practice, dedication, and a keen ear.

Good autoethnographers use dialogue as a way to advance character development, arguments, and story lines. Use it too much, and it will sound like you are using it as an exposition technique, as opposed to what you want it to be—a vibrant reflection of everyday life that, in this case, advances the story in important ways. The dialogue should flow as a central and driving force in the story.

For example, in my piece titled "Accidental Dialogue" (Poulos, 2008a), I chose to use a small conversation with my son, Noah, to illuminate how—given the right conditions and a certain kind of trusting relationship—genuine dialogue might just emerge spontaneously in everyday life. At the time, Noah was a precocious 10-year-old. After a long day of play, this kid tended to turn philosophical. This was not unusual for him. One evening, we were sitting by the fireplace after a long day of play.

NOAH: Matt says he's an atheist, but I don't believe him.

ME: Why do you say that?

NOAH: Because you can't just believe in nothing.

ME: Why not?

NOAH (an earnest look on his face): Even nothing is something.

ME: Yeah. Hmmm. What do you believe?

NOAH: Well, I believe in God, you know, but not like he's some guy up on a cloud or something. I think God just is.

ME (eyebrows raised): Wow. That's pretty cool. God is.

NOAH (smiles slightly): Yeah.

ME: So what's that mean?

NOAH: God is here. God's not away. It's *here.*

ME: Really?

NOAH: Well, something made all this. You know. It's like the lake. You just know it's beautiful, and it's a good place to be.

ME: Right. So. God is in the lake.

NOAH: Definitely. God is in the lake.

ME: Man, I love the lake.

NOAH: Yeah, me too. (pp. 120–121)

Immediately after this conversation, I wrote it in my field notes, as close to word-for-word as I could capture. And as I constructed the narrative, which is about dialogue in human life, I searched for, and crafted, the appropriate place for this little bit of conversation.

Or take this example, from H. L. Goodall, Jr.'s (2000) *Writing the New Ethnography,* in which he writes about observing two "mall rats" in action in a suburban mall:

"Like, wow, man . . . you *know*?"

"You bet, dude. These so-called *merchants* . . . heheh . . . these merchants, man, want us mall rats out of here."

"But they want our *money*, dude." The boy looks down and kicks at the floor. "It's just not fair."

"They just don't want us hanging around." A pause. "Walkin' around, like we do."

"*Check it out*, man. That fluff chick's hair is really *zooking*!" (p. 54)

Here Goodall used dialogue in the service of his story of becoming a genuine observer–participant–writer who can craft a vivid, striking tale that evokes the experience of everyday life in situ. It works mostly because it advances a narrative that sets up a reading of writing-as-praxis that captures some sort of spirit or essence of the lived experience of the author and the people among whom he finds himself. It also works because the dialogue is a direct reflection of how people actually talk—or at least how these people talk.

So, proceed with caution in writing dialogue. But by all means, proceed.

Build a Sense of Action

Sometimes the action in a story is simply talk, sometimes it is thought-as-action, sometimes it is moving through space and doing things. For example, this is an entry from my field notes on my days as a fencer:

We stand, facing one another, about fifteen feet apart, crisp white uniforms reflecting the fluorescent lights. We salute, our sabers swishing slightly, making their own little wind. We pull our masks on.

The referee calls out: "*En garde*."

Get ready.

We are ready.

"*Allez*!"

And we are charging at each other, full speed, sabers in motion.

Clang! Our sabers come together . . . and . . .

Something's wrong.

My hand.

I drop my saber, grab my hand. I look down at it, feeling the shock run up my arm, into my head. Blood is shooting out of a tiny hole in the back of my glove. I grab the glove, pull it off. Now the blood starts to spread more slowly, first across the back of my hand, then onto the palm. For some reason, I'm worried it will drip on the floor. I stare at my hand, unsure what's next, what should be next. I've never been stabbed before.

You are in the audience, watching a fencing match gone wrong. You see my hand bleeding, and you wonder whether it hurts, and if so, how much.

Attend to the Passage of Time

Because autoethnographers so often traffic in memory-as-data, autoethnographies are always moving around in time. We want to give our readers some direct sense of this traveling through and with time or of the passage of time or of the importance of time to the experience of being human. Sometimes we travel back 50 years:

> 1969 was a year for the ages. It was a year of openings, of breakthroughs, of turning points. In my own little corner of the world, it was a magical year. On the verge of my 11th birthday, I was hauling along (admittedly, on a purple one-speed Spider bike with a kick brake) toward that fabled time when I would come of age and go out into the world. Do you remember when you first became conscious of something changing in yourself, in your body, in your mind? Do you remember when you began to realize that one day you were not going to be a little kid anymore? Do you remember the first faint stirrings of love? Do you remember when you woke up to the music that shaped your generation? Do you remember when you first thought you might reach high, reach all the way to the moon? I do. (Poulos, 2016a, p. 1)

Sometimes, we flash back to yesterday or last week, or we flash forward 10 years, writing of an imagined future. The purpose of working with variations in time in a story is, as noted earlier, to show characters performing actions over some comprehensible span of time. Sometimes, we work against the conventions of linear time, and sometimes we play with the strange expansions and contractions of our collective experience of time. So, play around with time. But do it with purpose.

Evoke and Invoke Emotion

As an autoethnographer, I find myself striving to bring my emotions— from anger to sadness to joy to despair to ecstasy—to life on the page. This is where the writing takes on that magical quality of pure evocation, where writer and reader come together in an empathetic (feeling with) relationship.

As mentioned previously, in the academic year 2012–2013, seven of my closest friends and family members died in fairly rapid succession. As the first two deaths occurred, I wrote the following:

> We knew it was coming. But when it did, it seemed all too soon. Maybe you think you are ready for something like that. I think you never really are. And the pain of loss surges upward through my veins again. When Susan walks into the living room, she sees my wet eyes, knows immediately. "Bud?" she asks. I nod silently. A tear rolls down my cheek. I feel this loss down to my bones. That morning, as we walk our dogs around the neighborhood, we notice our beautiful border collie, Jake, now 13, is struggling. He has a hard time walking these days. He is arthritic, but something more intense seems wrong. Later in the day, we take a walk in our favorite park. A half-mile down the trail, Jake lies down. He is not walking any further. I lift his bony frame up and carry him back to the car. (Poulos, 2012c, p. 348)

Even as I read this short piece all these years later, a shudder rises through my body. And a tear rolls down my cheek, unbidden. And I grieve for the loss of all my friends, now nearly 7 years ago and for the loss of my dad, so very fresh indeed, and for all the losses everywhere. Grief and loss are central features of the human condition. Again, one purpose of autoethnographic writing is to move the reader into emotional identification, in the service of our ongoing conversation (social construction) of what it means to be human.

So far, I have advised you just to start writing but to do it with purpose and with a certain set of story-crafting conventions and considerations in mind (e.g., identification, vivid writing, character development and deployment, dialogue, action, time, emotion). But, of course, you may still be asking yourself (and me), How? Naturally, those of us who have been doing it for a while know a few secrets of writing in this way for academic and other audiences. As H. L. Goodall Jr. put it,

> To "write well" means that the writer adapts his or her material to a literary form consistent with the audience's expectations. Such adaptation in ethnography means that sentences are crafted out of the raw materials of remembered experiences, field notes, artifacts, and surmises, within an overall structure of meaning derived from the anticipation and satisfaction of the basic form. (2000, p. 73)

In autoethnography, readers expect to read a striking or evocative tale with a purpose. But how to put this into practice as you craft your sentences? You have to work at it, to be sure. And feel your way through.

Tie the Story to Theory

Your task as an autoethnographer is to make the aforementioned connections to the larger sociocultural matrix of human knowledge and experience within which your little slice of lived experience fits—and, naturally, to the theoretical traditions of your field of study. You will, therefore, spend considerable time building on the existing literature connected to the subject of your work, connecting your story to the ongoing cultural and academic and theoretical conversation about human life, then making broader connections beyond the existing literature. In autoethnography, as in life, practice informs theory, and theory informs practice. For example, I have used Jungian psychological theory and symbolic interactionist work to anchor a story of life in my complex, often dysfunctional, family of origin:

> To understand my story, you have to think first about the human shadow. Much has been written about this phenomenon, which Jung (1957, 1959, 1989) thought of as the "dark side" of the personal unconscious—the repressed, despised, misunderstood, disowned, and unwelcome parts of ourselves that reside somewhere just underneath the surface of the persona (face) that, under ordinary circumstances, we work hard put forth to the outer world. As Erving Goffman (1959, 1963, 1967) pointed out, much of our everyday communicative energy is aimed toward "face work"—the intricate and involved maintenance of a positive social image. But, of course, the fact that we work hard to present a positive "face" to the world does not negate the existence of our "dark side." The face can, in fact, easily fall under a shadow, and thus become disrupted. (Poulos, 2012a, p. 324)

This theoretical steering wheel assists me in my quest to understand my suffering, my family's suffering, and the suffering of countless families who fall into negative patterns of thinking and communicating imbued with the human shadow. In the piece, I go on to examine the stark and suffocating social pressures that emerge from a strong orientation toward the surveillance and impression management (face work) that comes with the role of a priest's family and the eruptions of anger (shadow) that can result from so much frustrating pursuit of the impossible (perfection). The framing discourse of Jungian and symbolic interactionist theory opens the door for the story to become something more than a mere story of a single family's dysfunction; infused with theory, it becomes a full-fledged autoethnography. So, as an autoethnographer, you should write a striking tale, to be sure, but you will also be called on to make sense of the story in some way.

Write Some Sort of Coda (Analysis or Interpretation)

In music, the *coda* is the last passage of a movement or piece, though, in musical forms such as jazz, it often blends right into the next movement or piece. Think of the coda of your autoethnography as the final words of this particular work, for now. You have to end somewhere. Like openings (invitations, hooks), closing paragraphs are crucial. This is where you leave the reader, move the reader to action, drive home the message of the story, craft some "last words" that show where you are in your thinking-feeling understanding of your lived experience at this moment in time, or just drop the reader off for some rumination. The coda is the space for (at least partial) interpretation. To accomplish this, integrate your practical and theoretical knowledge and write a coda, analysis, or interpretation that brings out the deeper contours of meaning in the story without hitting your reader over the head. The coda requires finesse; you should not be pedantic. You want your reader to think, feel, communicate, and go on about life changed in some way. Of course, it is up to you to carefully analyze and interpret your story within the frame of your discipline(s). Writing a strong coda is a way to engage your readers in an ongoing dialogue about the work. Most autoethnographers frame their stories with the relevant literature in the field of study and, in so doing, seek to make sense of the story, as I did in my research on family secrecy.

Write, Edit, Rewrite, Repeat

All good writing is the result of rewriting. I have already said a good deal about the craft of writing autoethnography and about the writing-rewriting-editing discipline of autoethnographic writing. For now, I will just reiterate that sentiment: Write, edit, rewrite, repeat.

5 VARIATIONS ON THE METHOD

As writer–researchers, autoethnographers are concerned with the rhythms, tones, and qualities of words, sentences, paragraphs, and stories. The rhythmic qualities of language set the tone for the piece and the experience of the reader. The rhythms and tones of your words and sentences must match the mood of the story. Will your story of grief be slow, rhythmic, like a mournful blues tune? Will your story of conflict be written in a staccato rhythm, like a driving rock song? Will your tortured memory be drawn into writing by a soulful jazz riff? Will your story of joy plink along the keys of life, like a sweet piano piece? How will you shape your words and sentences into rhythms, tones, and moods that evoke what you seek? Will you craft your research text in straight narrative prose, in poetry, as a layered account, as a performance script, as a collaborative work, as collage, or as a work of fiction?

Norman Denzin and Yvonna Lincoln (2005) advocated for a view of qualitative researchers as *bricoleurs* who assemble montages, collages, or bricolages, using various tools as a sort of "jack-of-all-trades" to piece together texts of various sorts designed to speak into the human conversation. They wrote, "The qualitative researcher may take on multiple and gendered images: scientist, naturalist, field-worker, journalist, social critic, artist, performer,

https://doi.org/10.1037/0000222-005
Essentials of Autoethnography, by C. N. Poulos

jazz musician, filmmaker, quilt maker, essayist" (p. 4). The notion of a bricoleur is appealing to those drawn to autoethnography, layered accounts, critical autoethnography, performance autoethnography, poetic inquiry, and other forms, all conceived of as creative methods to build social research texts.

The many variations on autoethnographic writing-as-inquiry offer a wide array of approaches and pathways to be pursued, driven always by the nature of the research, the questions being explored, and the way the story has to emerge given the situation at hand. This creative realm of qualitative inquiry is a rich field of endeavor that holds great promise for those inclined to attend to the ways readers and audiences can be deeply engaged and their thinking transformed. The following are some of the many variations of this method of writing-as-inquiry. The potential variations constitute important decisions that shape the way your text will work on readers and point to the possibilities of creative choices in using this vibrant research method. In recent years, researchers have experimented with and developed genre variations, such as layered accounts, critical autoethnography, performance autoethnography, poetic inquiry, collaborative autoethnography and duoethnography, and so on.

LAYERED ACCOUNTS

Carol Rambo Ronai (1995) first experimented with the layered approach in her early autoethnographic stories of childhood abuse and trauma. A *layered account* weaves the author's various voices (subject positions, roles, or perspectives) into a text with layers that enrich the work with a multivocal and multiperspectival quality and then allows the researcher to compare or examine how various layers or perspectives connect. As she put it, such an approach enables ethnographers to break out of conventional writing formats by integrating abstract theoretical material with "layered" accounts of experience—in her case, from her positions as a child sexual abuse survivor, academic sociologist, adult in therapy, and so on—offering "an impressionistic sketch, handing readers layers of experience so they may fill in the spaces and construct an interpretation of the writer's narrative" (p. 396). The text reads like a conversation between her academic self, her childhood self, and her therapy patient self (with each of the "layers" or perspectives given voice). She goes on to show how the multiple ways of accounting for experience can "speak" to each other and readers in a way other forms of writing cannot. Similarly, Fox (1996) experimented with "layers" of the various voices involved in a child sexual abuse case—crafting an imagined "conversation" between the abuser, victim, and researcher—leaving the reader with impressions but few conclusions.

CRITICAL AUTOETHNOGRAPHY

In *Critical Autoethnography: Intersecting Cultural Identities in Everyday Life*, Robin Boylorn and Mark Orbe (2016) wrote of *critical autoethnography* as "cultural analysis through personal narrative" written through "a critical lens" (p. 17). Critical autoethnography intensifies and directs the writing in a critical (rather than purely interpretive) direction to serve up a cultural critique of power, hegemony, hierarchy, and so on. Critical autoethnography proceeds from an essentially democratic viewpoint that drives the work toward offering solutions to problems of inequality; democratic participation; workplace, community, or institutional inequity; and so on. Critical autoethnography brings critical theory—a philosophical approach to culture that interrogates ideology, power, and the structural constraints of actors in a cultural system (e.g., oppression)—into direct conversation with audiences through autoethnographic texts.

Critical theories of race, gender, sexuality, and so on, emerge through autoethnographies of marginalized voices and people. Powerful critical autoethnographic works have emerged in recent years, offering social critiques from feminist (Ettorre, 2016; S. Faulkner, 2018), Blackgirl and feminist (Boylorn, 2016; Cooper et al., 2017), Black male and queer (Alexander, 2006, 2012), Indigenous (Iosefo, 2014), postcolonial (Fitzpatrick, 2018), disabled (Scott, 2019; Scott & Houtzer, 2018), and queer (Adams, 2011) standpoints, to name just a few.

PERFORMANCE AUTOETHNOGRAPHY

Tami Spry (2011) advocated writing autoethnography with the goal of embodied performance in mind—to bring the text to embodied and physical life. That is, we seek to craft and then embody our work by performing it for audiences; in turn, our work is driven with the performative imperative in mind. Hearkening back to the work of phenomenologists (see Merelau-Ponty's integrative work on embodied perception: "I *am* my body!"—1962, p. 198), Spry argued that "autoethnography is body and verse" (p. 15) and that we should turn ourselves toward what Dwight Conquergood (1998) referred to as "performance-sensitive ways of knowing" (p. 26)—that is, ways of knowing and showing that document and perform how human being is evoked and embodied in and through performance. Performance studies has a long tradition in the discipline of communication studies, and autoethnographic performances are often staged by performance studies scholars. Scholars such as Tami Spry, Craig Gingrich-Philbrook, Lesa Lockford, Ron Pelias, Elyse Pineau, Julie-Ann Scott-Pollock, Ann Harris, Stacy Holman Jones, Tracy Stephenson Shaffer, Bryant Keith Alexander, and others regularly write and perform—or have their students perform—autoethnographic performance texts as staged shows for public consumption.

POETIC INQUIRY

Autoethnographers who are poetically inclined use poetry and poetic language to accomplish things straight prose cannot, speak about issues in ways that step away from straight narrative, or accomplish poetic rather than narrative ends. There are too many examples to list them all here. Sandra Faulkner (2019) has written extensively about the methodology of poetic inquiry as a research practice, weaving autoethnography and poetry together to build a critical social justice research agenda. Pelias (2004, 2011), has written poetically about a poetics of personal relations, showing forth how close relationships are built through communicative acts. Boylorn (2012), Tillmann (2009), Weems (2008), and others have used poetry to highlight, bridge, sharpen, or soften and speak into the liminal spaces between everyday life and transcendent experience to point out injustice or speak truth to power. Many other autoethnographers are experimenting with poetry to speak into the nearly ineffable, liminal spaces between thoughts, words, and experience. All are using words in creative, evocative, poetic ways to get at the heart of the questions they are pursuing.

For example, Mohan Dutta and Ambar Basu (2013) used poetry to highlight the experience of being an "other" in a Eurocentric world. The following is the opening:

> I am a brown man
> Primitive, backward, insolent
> I have for generations
> Hated my brownness (Dutta & Basu, 2013, p. 147)

Writing poetically of this "erasure" as a human being against a hegemonic background offers a way for us to "see into" the author's point of view. Marilyn Metta (2013) wrote her way through domestic violence, weaving together poetry, prose, and drawings to evoke what it is like to suffer at the hands of a sexual predator:

> She shivers in shame as
> A feast of porn feeds the beast
> Merely a piece of red meat
> Upon which his selfish desires feast (p. 486)

Writing this way allows the autoethnographer to offer a glimpse into her world and to write in a different voice, way, and rhythm, vividly evoking the deeper contours of experience.

AUTOETHNOGRAPHY AS SOCIAL FICTION

Hearkening back to the existentialists, who produced philosophical works as fiction (see Chapter 1), Patricia Leavy (2013, 2015) has been a leader in advocating for, writing, and publishing fictional works (short stories, novellas, and novels) that offer another alternative form of qualitative inquiry that, like autoethnography, emphasizes writing as research practice. She argued, "Using fiction as a social research practice is a natural extension of what many researchers and writers have long been doing" (Leavy, 2013, p. 20). The arts-based research movement in qualitative inquiry has adapted tools and practices of the creative arts—methods that "can be used in all phases of social research" (Leavy, 2013, p. 22). The primary notion here is that creative works such as novels offer compelling ways to craft research-based texts that appeal to broader audiences than a standard or traditional research report. Reading this paragraph, you may not buy that this work can be legitimate research. I urge you to suspend judgment and read some of Leavy's award-winning work.

COLLABORATIVE AUTOETHNOGRAPHY

Autoethnographers generally produce solo-authored texts, with rare exceptions. There are, however, autoethnographers and performative writers who have experimented with writing teams in recent years and set off growing interest in collaborative coauthored dialogic-responsive autoethnographic texts (Gale et al., 2012) and with what Diversi and Moreira (2009, 2018) called "duoethnography," in which multiple authors write about a question or prompt or build on each other's writing in dialogue. These texts are written collaboratively and responsively (to each other and to imagined readers) from the points of view of the various authors. This newer variation on autoethnographic writing shows great promise as more teams of scholars are gathering to produce coauthored multivocal texts.

Thin traces of memory arise as I recall Jonathan Wyatt and Ken Gale performing a collaborative autoethnography at the International Congress of Qualitative Inquiry. I tracked it down in the *Handbook of Autoethnography* (Jones et al., 2013):

> *As we align our relational ontologies in particular ways . . .*
> *A plea for autoethnography as "co-presence with others . . ."*
> Writing has never seemed more difficult. It has never seemed more dangerous.
> Writing *does*. It changes how things are, how I see the world . . .
> *A new vector of becoming.* (Wyatt & Gale, 2013, p. 302, italics in original)

For more variations on approaches to writing autoethnography, see the list of exemplars in the appendix at the end of this text. Of particular note are several newer works listed there, by Dunn (2018), Paxton (2018), and Wyatt (2018).

6 METHODOLOGICAL INTEGRITY, SUMMARY, AND CONCLUSIONS

Sarah J. Tracy (2010) offered eight big tent criteria for evaluating all qualitative research. Does the work show that it satisfies engagement with and is characterized by (a) a worthy topic, (b) rich rigor, (c) sincerity, (d) credibility, (e) resonance, (f) a significant contribution, (g) an ethical approach, and (h) meaningful coherence? Tracy's approach offers a useful doorway for all qualitative researchers to hone their craft toward what she calls "qualitative quality" (p. 837) and for readers to consider the value and impact of any qualitative text. Autoethnography, when done well, can be read as satisfying all these criteria, though no list of criteria can capture or contain all the varied contours and forms of autoethnographic work, nor can all works be said to satisfy all of them. We may want to read these "criteria" as guideposts rather than absolutes.

In their discussions of ensuring methodological alignment with American Psychological Association (2018) reporting standards and methodological integrity in qualitative research, Levitt et al. (2017) and Levitt et al. (2018) defined methodological integrity as alignment between decisions about methodological choices:

> Integrity is established when *research designs and procedures* [emphasis added] (e.g., autoethnography, discursive analysis) support the *research goals* [emphasis added] (i.e., the research problems/questions); respect the researcher's *approaches*

https://doi.org/10.1037/0000222-006
Essentials of Autoethnography, by C. N. Poulos

to inquiry [emphasis added] (i.e., research traditions sometimes described as world views, paradigms, or philosophical/epistemological assumptions) and are tailored for *fundamental characteristics of subject matter and investigators* [emphasis added]. (Levitt et al., 2017, pp. 9–10)

Further, they ground their talk of methodological integrity in standards of trustworthiness, fidelity, and utility—common ways of thinking about qualitative research. *Trustworthiness*, in autoethnography, is often driven by the ethos of the author, who shows forth self in the manuscript in ways that reveal credibility and build identification between reader and author. The degree to which readers (including other researchers) are persuaded that a study captures a significant experience is largely dependent on the quality of the writing and the emergent credibility (ethos) of the author. *Fidelity*, in autoethnography, arises out of the immersion of the author in a slice of the lifeworld and the depth, quality, and intensity of the written evocation of lived experience. *Utility*, in autoethnography, is seen as a product of how well the author renders deep, rich, evocative, compelling, striking tales that lead to profound answers to important questions—or the emergence of additional important questions.

EVALUATING AUTOETHNOGRAPHY

In other words, when you attempt to write autoethnography (as with any qualitative research), you should ensure alignment between research questions, approaches and procedures, research goals, and the subject matter of research (including self) and offer up trustworthy, faithful, and useful work. Having emphasized so strongly the centrality of writing to autoethnographic inquiry, I must add here that autoethnographers must write vivid, evocative, striking tales of human social life. Perhaps the best model for evaluating the quality and integrity of autoethnography comes from the work of Laurel Richardson (2000):

1. *Substantive contribution*: Does this piece contribute to our understanding of social life? Does the writer demonstrate a deeply grounded (if embedded) human-world understanding and perspective? How has this perspective informed the construction of the text?

2. *Aesthetic merit*: Does this piece succeed aesthetically? Does the use of creative analytical practices open up the text, invite interpretive responses? Is the text artistically shaped, satisfying, complex, and not boring?

3. *Reflexivity*: How did the author come to write this text? How was the information gathered? How has the author's subjectivity been both a producer and a product of this text? Is there adequate self-awareness and self-exposure

for the reader to make judgments about the point of view? Do authors hold themselves accountable to the standards of knowing and telling of the people they have studied?

4. *Impact*: Does this text affect me? Emotionally? Intellectually? Generate new questions? Move me to write? Move me to try new research practices? Move me to action?

5. *Expresses a reality*: Does this text embody a fleshed out, embodied sense of lived experience? Does it seem "true"—a credible account of a cultural, social, individual, or communal sense of the "real"? (p. 254)

In my work on evaluating autoethnography (Poulos, 2013), I offered a series of "touchstones" for how reviewers of this work ought to consider and evaluate the value of what they are reading. These reviewer touchstones can be useful for the writer of autoethnography. Knowing what a reviewer might look for can help a writer construct a text that "works." These touchstones should seem familiar because many of them simply reinforce or extend points I've made in previous chapters:

1. The experience of the ethnographer is central to the construction of the text. The autoethnographer embraces subjectivity as a vital mover of human social action. "Data collection" prominently focuses on introspection and writing about the personal experience of the researcher.

2. Autoethnography is not "merely" the rendering of the author's experience, however; it seeks to link the personal to the larger cultural, social, political, and academic world-matrix in which the autoethnographer participates.

3. Autoethnographic writing is aimed at crafting evocative, compelling, emotionally and intellectually rich tales that draw the reader into the lifeworld of the researcher.

4. Autoethnography proceeds from an assumption that moving or changing/ transforming both author and reader (emotionally, intellectually, actively) is a primary aim of research.

5. The autoethnographer writes with "heart" as well as "head."

6. Autoethnographies are grounded in a theory of knowledge that is reflexive, phenomenological and *praxis*-driven (i.e., grounded in and driven by action, performance, accomplishment), and built out of *phrônesis* (practical-moral wisdom; ethical knowing).

7. Autoethnography proceeds as an interpretive/critical process. (Poulos, 2013, pp. 45–47)

Further guidance on evaluating autoethnography can be found in the *Handbook of Autoethnography* (Jones et al., 2013), particularly in the "framing" chapters written by Adams, Ellis, Holman Jones, Bochner, Goodall, Tedlock, and Sparkes. By following these frameworks and the guidance of experienced autoethnographers, authors can ensure that the work will be carefully attuned to the various concerns and standards readers and reviewers in the autoethnographic community may be applying to its evaluation, and readers can assess the quality and import of the work.

Further, to show methodological integrity, autoethnographers often focus attention directly on the approaches to inquiry taken in the work. The research designs, procedures, goals, and the characteristics of the subject and author are sometimes attended to explicitly in a methodological statement of some sort; at other times, these assumptions are embedded in the narrative. Because writing-as-inquiry drives the work, how quality is demonstrated may vary widely, depending on the structure and goals of the piece and the standards of the publication outlet.

Bochner (2000) and Gingrich-Philbrook (2013) offered strong, cogent critiques of criteria, evaluators, and evaluations in the domain of narrative work. Perhaps it's time to let go, read openly, and allow the work to work on you. Does the work engage you? Maybe that is enough.

ETHICS

Most commentators on the ethics of autoethnography have urged that a relational ethic of care and compassion drive the work, especially when other humans are either included or mentioned in the work (Ellis, 2004, 2009/2020; Poulos, 2008b). The ethical impulse to "do no harm" guides the crafting of the work. In his book *Searching for an Autoethnographic Ethic*, Stephen Andrew (2017) offered extended consideration to how to build an ethical framework for doing autoethnography. He searched for a way to use "intuitionism" (the idea that we already intuitively know what we ought to do) as a philosophical basis for approaching the ethics of autoethnographic writing. He offered a pathway to reading the ethical implications of autoethnography via ethical intentions, exposure to ethical compromise or harm, and duty to self, others, and readers. Tullis (2013) laid out specific ethical guidelines for autoethnographers, focusing attention on informed consent and the protection of self and others. The bottom line here is that we strive to practice peaceful, non-harming action in and through our writing. Autoethnographers must, in the end, build a consciousness of the ways the work may (or may not) cause harm to self and others. It is an open, heartfelt form of writing that exposes all sorts of vulnerabilities. There is no simple answer to such questions, but most autoethnographers direct their attention to ethical considerations as they craft their texts.

SUMMARY AND CONCLUSIONS

Autoethnography is a powerful way to craft a striking story, dig deep, evoke the richness of the lifeworld of researchers and participants, offer a cultural critique from a specific standpoint, open up worldviews, and engage the hearts of readers. At its best, autoethnography stuns (or at least provokes) the reader—into deeply felt emotion, silence, action, questioning, vibrant conversation, deep reflection, and embracing life at its fullest, richest, most painful, and most ecstatic. It is fundamentally disruptive (Poulos, 2004). That said, reading and writing autoethnography is not for the faint of heart. Brace yourself.

I will say this: My career as an autoethnographer has been both risky and rewarding beyond my wildest dreams. I have written my way through a lot of tight spots. Consider how poignantly Emmanuel Levinas (1998) pointed out the risks of vulnerability in communication: "Communication with the other can be transcendent only as a *dangerous* life, a fine risk to be run" (p. 120). It is a dangerous life indeed, opening up my vulnerability as I put myself out there for the other humans I communicate with (my readers). The biggest risk, by far, is this: The deep emotional introspection associated with this form of academic writing comes with inherent vulnerability and exposure to the judgment of others, along with the possibility of opening up old trauma, stirring up painful memories, digging into taboo subjects, or sparking grief or other deep emotions. So, the writer (and the reader) should proceed with caution and take care of their emotional states. Another risk that is often overlooked is that this work is hard. Writing is difficult. Writing well—writing beautifully, that is—is much harder than most people think.

Along with the risks, of course, are the standard cautionary notes. If you want to build predictive models or produce generalizable knowledge, you're barking up the wrong tree here. If you want statistics, you'll have to look elsewhere. If you are irritated by those who write in the first person, you're not going to like autoethnography. Of course, if that's the case, I doubt you have read this far in this book. If you want work that produces overarching grand theories, you are not likely to find it here.

When asked to point out the weaknesses of the method, most autoethnographers will say that its biggest weakness is also its biggest strength. The charge that autoethnography is just one person's perspective is, of course, true. But one person's perspective can be powerful, moving, and transformative—and, in the end, we all work from our own perspective. The question is this: Does autoethnography speak to you? If it does, it has touched on something in our common humanity. And that is something.

Of course, I believe that these risks and drawbacks and limitations are easily overtaken by the rewards of autoethnography. If you want a deeper look into the questions that humans raise about what it means to be one of us, in relationships, communities, a culture, autoethnography might be just the ticket. If you are searching for rich, evocative, moving, striking academic writing replete with vivid, thick description and infused with powerful emotion, autoethnography might be just what you are looking for. If you want to read and write work that breaks your heart, autoethnography is a poignant, powerful path to follow.

If you want to read and write work that dares to tread into territory others have feared to enter, autoethnography is likely already there. If you want to read and write work that deals with issues that cannot be grasped by methods divorced from human engagement and emotion, autoethnography will take you there. Indeed, I like to think there are many benefits to reading and writing autoethnography. Among these are the sheer joy of reading and writing excellent words as they work their magic on the page. There are few pleasures greater than reading a striking, startling story. How much academic writing can you say that about? This is writing that will move you. This is writing that will catalyze action. This is writing that will provoke you. This is writing that will break your heart. This is writing that will stir you to great joy. This is writing that will shake you to your core. This is writing that will spark creativity. This is writing that will stun you. This is writing that will take your breath away.

It is my fervent hope that reading this volume will entice you to at least attempt autoethnography, assuming it aligns well with your questions, your goals, and the subject(s) of your research agenda. I leave you with this challenge: Start writing. Then edit, rewrite, and repeat.

Appendix

EXEMPLAR STUDIES

Adams, T. E. (2011). *Narrating the closet: An autoethnography of same-sex attrac-tion.* Routledge.

Bochner, A. P., & Ellis, C. (Eds.). (2002). *Ethnographically speaking: Autoethnog-raphy, literature, and aesthetics.* AltaMira Press.

Boylorn, R. M. (2012). *Sweetwater: Black women and narratives of resilience.* Peter Lang.

Dunn, T. R. (2018). *Talking white trash: Mediated representations and lived experi-ences of white working-class people.* Routledge.

Ellis, C. (1995). *Final negotiations: A story of love, loss, and chronic illness.* Temple University Press.

Ellis, C. (2004). *The ethnographic I: A methodological novel about autoethnography.* AltaMira Press.

Goodall, H. L., Jr. (1989). *Casing a promised land: The autobiography of an orga-nizational detective as cultural ethnographer.* Southern Illinois University Press.

Goodall, H. L., Jr. (1996). *Divine signs: Connecting spirit to community.* Southern Illinois University Press.

Jones, S. H., Adams, T. E., & Ellis, C. (Eds.). (2013). *Handbook of autoethnography.* Left Coast Press.

Paxton, B. (2018). *At home with grief: Continued bonds with the deceased.* Routledge.

Pelias, R. J. (2004). *A methodology of the heart: Evoking academic and daily life.* AltaMira Press.

Pelias, R. J. (2011). *Leaning: A poetics of personal relations.* Left Coast Press.

Poulos, C. N. (2019). *Accidental ethnography: An inquiry into family secrecy.* Routledge.

Wyatt, J. (2018). *Therapy, stand-up, and the gesture of writing: Towards creative-relational inquiry.* Routledge.

References

Adams, T. E. (2011). *Narrating the closet: An autoethnography of same-sex attraction*. Routledge.

Adams, T. E., Jones, S. H., & Ellis, C. (2015). *Autoethnography: Understanding qualitative research*. Oxford University Press.

Alexander, B. K. (2006). *Performing black masculinity: Race, culture, and queer identity*. AltaMira Press.

Alexander, B. K. (2012). *The performative sustainability of race: Reflections on black culture and the politics of identity*. Peter Lang.

American Psychological Association. (2018). *APA Style journal article reporting standards*. https://www.apa.org/pubs/journals/resources/apa-style-jars

Andrew, S. (2017). *Searching for an autoethnographic ethic*. Routledge.

Baglia, J. (2019). Beginning again: Diagnosis as breach, survival as a new normal. In L. W. Peterson & C. E. Kiesinger (Eds.), *Narrating midlife: Crisis, transition, and transformation* (pp. 107–130). Lexington Books.

Bakhtin, M. M. (1993). *Toward a philosophy of the act* (V. Liapunov, Trans.). University of Texas Press.

Behar, R. (1996). *The vulnerable observer: Anthropology that breaks your heart*. Beacon Press.

Berger, P. L., & Luckmann, T. (1966). *The social construction of reality: A treatise in the sociology of knowledge*. Anchor Books.

Berry, K. (2016). *Bullied: Tales of torment, identity, and youth*. Routledge.

Black, C. (1985). *Repeat after me*. Hazelden.

Black, C. (2002). *It will never happen to me: Growing up with addiction as youngsters, adolescents, adults*. Hazelden.

Blumer, H. (1969). *Symbolic interactionism: Perspective and method*. Prentice-Hall. (Original work published 1931)

Bochner, A. P. (2000). Criteria against ourselves. *Qualitative Inquiry, 6*(2), 266–272. https://doi.org/10.1177/107780040000600209

Bochner, A. P. (2001). Narrative's virtues. *Qualitative Inquiry, 7*(2), 131–157. https://doi.org/10.1177/107780040100700201

Bochner, A. P., & Ellis, C. (1992). Personal narrative as a social approach to interpersonal communication. *Communication Theory, 2*(2), 165–172. https://doi.org/10.1111/j.1468-2885.1992.tb00036.x

Boylorn, R. M. (2012). *Sweetwater: Black women and narratives of resilience.* Peter Lang.

Boylorn, R. M. (2016). On being at home with myself: Blackgirl autoethnography as research praxis. *International Review of Qualitative Research, 9*(1), 44–58. https://doi.org/10.1525/irqr.2016.9.1.44

Boylorn, R. M., & Orbe, M. P. (Eds.). (2016). *Critical autoethnography: Intersecting cultural identities in everyday life.* Routledge. https://doi.org/10.4324/9781315431253

Bradshaw, J. (1995). *Family secrets: The path to self-acceptance and reunion.* Bantam Books.

Campbell, J. (1949). *The hero with a thousand faces.* Princeton University Press.

Camus, A. (1955). *The myth of Sisyphus and other essays.* Random House.

Chester, D. H. (2003). Mother/unmother: A storied look at infertility, identity, and transformation. *Qualitative Inquiry, 9*(5), 774–784. https://doi.org/10.1177/1077800403254887

Conquergood, D. (1998). Beyond the text: Toward a performative cultural politics. In S. J. Dailey (Ed.), *The future of performance studies: Visions and revisions* (pp. 25–36). NCA.

Cooley, C. H. (1998). *On self and social organization.* University of Chicago Press. (Original work published 1909)

Cooper, B. C., Morris, S. M., & Boylorn, R. M. (Eds.). (2017). *The crunk feminist collection.* The Feminist Press.

Denzin, N. K. (1989). *Interpretive biography.* SAGE. https://doi.org/10.4135/9781412984584

Denzin, N. K., & Lincoln, Y. S. (Eds.). (2005). *The Sage handbook of qualitative research* (2nd ed.). SAGE.

Derrida, J. (1974). *Of grammatology.* Johns Hopkins University Press. (Original work published 1967)

Diversi, M., & Moreira, C. (2009). *Betweener talk: Decolonizing knowledge production, pedagogy, and praxis.* Routledge.

Diversi, M., & Moreira, C. (2018). *Betweener autoethnographies: A path towards social justice.* Routledge. https://doi.org/10.4324/9780203711996

Dostoevsky, F. (1994). *Notes from underground.* Vintage. (Original work published 1864)

Dunn, T. R. (2018). *Talking white trash: Mediated representations and lived experiences of white working-class people.* Routledge. https://doi.org/10.4324/9781351045759

Dutta, M. J., & Basu, A. (2013). Negotiating our postcolonial selves from the ground to the ivory tower. In S. H. Jones, T. E. Adams, & C. E. Ellis (Eds.), *Handbook of autoethnography* (pp. 143–161). Left Coast Press.

Eisenberg, E. M. (1990). Jamming: Transcendence through organizing. *Communication Research, 17*(2), 139–164. https://doi.org/10.1177/009365090017002001

Ellis, C. (1991). Sociological introspection and emotional experience. *Symbolic Interaction, 14*(1), 23–50. https://doi.org/10.1525/si.1991.14.1.23

Ellis, C. (1995). *Final negotiations: A story of love, loss, and chronic illness.* Temple University Press.

Ellis, C. (2004). *The ethnographic I: A methodological novel about autoethnography.* AltaMira Press.

Ellis, C. (2020). *Revision: Autoethnographic reflections on life and work.* Routledge. (Original work published 2009)

Ellis, C., Adams, T. E., & Bochner, A. P. (2011). Autoethnography: An overview. *Historical Social Research, 36,* 273–290.

Ellis, C., & Bochner, A. P. (1991). Telling and performing personal stories: The constraints of choice in abortion. In C. Ellis & M. G. Flaherty (Eds.), *Investigating subjectivity: Research on lived experience* (pp. 79–101). SAGE.

The Ethnogs, Fem Nogs, & Rip Tupp. (2011). Performing mythic identity: An analysis and critique of "The Ethnogs." *Qualitative Inquiry, 17*(7), 664–674. https://doi.org/10.1177/1077800411414008

Ettorre, E. (2016). *Autoethnography as feminist method: Sensitising the feminist 'I.'* Routledge. https://doi.org/10.4324/9781315626819

Faulkner, S. L. (2018). *Real women run: Running as feminist embodiment.* Routledge. https://doi.org/10.4324/9781315437859

Faulkner, S. L. (2019). *Poetic inquiry as social justice and political response.* Vernon Press. https://doi.org/10.4324/9781351044233

Faulkner, W. (1990). *The sound and the fury.* Vintage. (Original work published 1929)

Fisher, W. K. (1985). The narrative paradigm: In the beginning. *Journal of Communication, 35*(4), 74–89. https://doi.org/10.1111/j.1460-2466.1985.tb02974.x

Fitzpatrick, E. (2018). A story of becoming: Entanglement, settler ghosts, and postcolonial counterstories. *Cultural Studies ↔ Critical Methodologies, 18*(1), 43–51.

Fox, K. V. (1996). Silent voices: A subversive reading of child sexual abuse. In C. Ellis & A. P. Bochner (Eds.), *Composing ethnography: Alternative forms of qualitative writing* (pp. 330–356). AltaMira Press.

Gale, K., Pelias, R. J., Russell, L., Spry, T., & Wyatt, J. (2012). *How writing touches: An intimate scholarly collaboration.* Cambridge Scholars Publishing.

Geertz, C. (1973). *The interpretation of cultures.* Basic Books.

Gergen, K. J. (1992). *The saturated self.* Basic Books.

Gergen, K. J. (2009). *Relational being: Beyond self and community.* Oxford University Press.

Giddens, A. (1984). *The constitution of society.* University of California Press.

Gingrich-Philbrook, C. (2013). Evaluating (evaluations of) autoethnography. In S. H. Jones, T. E. Adams, & C. E. Ellis (Eds.), *Handbook of autoethnography* (pp. 609–626). Left Coast Press.

Goffman, E. (1959). *The presentation of self in everyday life.* Doubleday.

Goffman, E. (1963). *Stigma: Notes on the management of spoiled identity.* Simon & Schuster.

Goffman, E. (1967). *Interaction ritual: Essays on face-to-face behavior.* Pantheon.

Goodall, H. L., Jr. (1989). *Casing a promised land: The autobiography of an organizational detective as cultural ethnographer.* Southern Illinois University Press.

Goodall, H. L., Jr. (1991). *Living in the rock n roll mystery: Reading context, self, and others as clues.* Southern Illinois University Press.

Goodall, H. L., Jr. (1996). *Divine signs: Connecting spirit to community.* Southern Illinois University Press.

Goodall, H. L., Jr. (2000). *Writing the new ethnography.* AltaMira Press.

Goodall, H. L., Jr. (2005). Narrative inheritance: A nuclear family with toxic secrets. *Qualitative Inquiry, 11*(4), 492–513. https://doi.org/10.1177/1077800405276769

Goodall, H. L., Jr. (2007). *Writing qualitative inquiry: Self, stories, & academic life.* Left Coast Press.

Heidegger, M. (2010). *Being and time* (J. Stambaugh, Trans.). SUNY Press. (Original work published 1953)

Hunniecutt, J. (2018). *Rethinking reintegration and veteran identity: A new consciousness* [Doctoral dissertation, University of Denver]. University of Denver Digital Commons. https://digitalcommons.du.edu/etd/1464

Hymes, D. (1962). The ethnography of speaking. In T. Gladwin & W. C. Sturtevant (Eds.), *Anthropology and human behavior* (pp. 13–53). Anthropology Society of Washington.

Iosefo, J. O. (2014). *Moonwalking with the Pasifika Girl in the Mirror: An autoethnography on spaces in higher education.* The University of Auckland.

Jones, S. H., Adams, T. E., & Ellis, C. (Eds.). (2013). *Handbook of autoethnography.* Left Coast Press.

Kafka, F. (2012). *The trial.* Schocken. (Original work published 1925)

Keen, S. (1992). *Fire in the belly: On being a man.* Bantam Books.

Kierkegaard, S. (1980). *The sickness unto death* (H. V. Hong & E. H. Hong, Trans.). Princeton University Press. (Original work published 1849)

Kuhn, A. (1995). *Family secrets: Acts of memory and imagination.* Verso.

Lamott, A. (1995). *Bird by bird: Some instructions on writing and life.* Anchor Books.

Leavy, P. (2013). *Fiction as research practice: Short stories, novellas, and novels.* Routledge.

Leavy, P. (2015). *Low-fat love.* Sense Publishers.

Lévi-Strauss, C. (1963). *Structural anthropology.* Basic Books.

Levinas, E. (1998). *Otherwise than being or beyond essence* (A. Lingis, Trans.). Duquesne University Press.

Levitt, H. M., Bamberg, M., Creswell, J. W., Frost, D. M., Josselson, R., & Suárez-Orozco, C. (2018). Journal article reporting standards for qualitative primary, qualitative meta-analytic, and mixed methods research in psychology: The APA Publications and Communications Board task force report. *American Psychologist, 73*(1), 26–46. https://doi.org/10.1037/amp0000151

Levitt, H. M., Wertz, F. J., Motulsky, S. L., Morrow, S. L., & Ponterotto, J. G. (2017). Recommendations for designing and reviewing qualitative research in psychology: Promoting methodological integrity. *Qualitative Psychology, 4*(1), 2–22. https://doi.org/10.1037/qup0000082

Lyotard, J.-F. (1979). *The postmodern condition: A report on knowledge*. University of Minnesota Press.

Malinowski, B. (1967). *A diary in the strict sense of the term*. Harcourt, Brace & World.

Marcel, G. (1960). *The mystery of being*. Regnery Press.

May, R. (1991). *The cry for myth*. Norton.

McGlashan, A. (1986). The translucence of memory. *Parabola: Myth and the quest for meaning, 11*(4), 6–11.

McGlashan, A. (1988). *The savage and beautiful country*. Daimon Verlag.

Mead, G. H. (1934). *Mind, self & society*. The University of Chicago Press.

Merleau-Ponty, M. (1962). *Phenomenology of perception*. Routledge and Kegan Paul.

Metta, M. (2013). Putting the body on the line: Embodied writing and recovery through domestic violence. In S. H. Jones, T. E. Adams, & C. E. Ellis (Eds.), *Handbook of autoethnography* (pp. 486–509). Left Coast Press.

Moreland, R. C. (Ed.). (2007). *A companion to William Faulkner*. Blackwell.

Nietzsche, F. (2006). *The will to power*. Barnes & Noble. (Original work published 1968)

Olt, P. A. (2018). Through army-colored glasses: A layered account of one veteran's experiences in higher education. *Qualitative Report, 23*, 2403–2421.

Osherson, S. (2001). *Finding our fathers: How a man's life is shaped by his relationship with his father*. McGraw-Hill.

Otto, R. (1958). *The idea of the holy: An inquiry into the nonrational factor in the idea of the divine and its relation to the rational* (J. W. Harvey, Trans.). Oxford University Press.

Paxton, B. (2018). *At home with grief: Continued bonds with the deceased*. Routledge.

Pelias, R. J. (2004). *A methodology of the heart: Evoking academic and daily life*. AltaMira Press.

Pelias, R. J. (2011). *Leaning: A poetics of personal relations*. Left Coast Press.

Percy, W. (1960). *The moviegoer*. Alfred A. Knopf.

Percy, W. (1971). *Love in the ruins*. Farrar, Strauss & Giroux.

Percy, W. (1991). *Signposts in a strange land*. Farrar, Strauss & Giroux.

Philipsen, G. (1992). *Speaking culturally*. SUNY Press.

Poulos, C. N. (2004). Disruption, silence, and creation: The search for dialogic civility in the age of anxiety. *Qualitative Inquiry, 10*(4), 534–547. https://doi.org/10.1177/1077800403257679

Poulos, C. N. (2008a). Accidental dialogue: The search for dialogic moments in everyday life. *Communication Theory, 18*(1), 117–138. https://doi.org/10.1111/j.1468-2885.2007.00316.x

Poulos, C. N. (2008b). Narrative conscience and the autoethnographic adventure: Probing memories, secrets, shadows, and possibilities. *Qualitative Inquiry, 14*(1), 46–66. https://doi.org/10.1177/1077800407308916

Poulos, C. N. (2012a). Life, interrupted. *Qualitative Inquiry, 18*(4), 323–332. https://doi.org/10.1177/1077800411431565

Poulos, C. N. (2012b). Stumbling into relating: Writing a relationship with my father. *Qualitative Inquiry, 18*(2), 197–202. https://doi.org/10.1177/1077800411429099

Poulos, C. N. (2012c). Writing through the memories: Autoethnography as a path to transcendence. *International Review of Qualitative Research, 5*(3), 315–326. https://doi.org/10.1525/irqr.2012.5.3.315

Poulos, C. N. (2013). Autoethnography. In A. Trainor & E. Graue (Eds.), *Reviewing qualitative research in the social and behavioral sciences: A guide for reviewers and researchers* (pp. 38–53). Routledge.

Poulos, C. N. (2014). Writing a bridge to possibility. *International Review of Qualitative Research, 7*(3), 342–358. https://doi.org/10.1525/irqr.2014.7.3.342

Poulos, C. N. (2016a). An autoethnography of memory and connection. *Qualitative Inquiry, 22*(7), 552–558. https://doi.org/10.1177/1077800415622506

Poulos, C. N. (2016b). Evocative writing. In C. Davis & R. Potter (Eds.), *International encyclopedia of communication research methods* (pp. 1–7). Wiley-Blackwell. https://doi.org/10.1002/9781118901731.iecrm0094

Poulos, C. N. (2019). *Accidental ethnography: An inquiry into family secrecy*. Routledge.

Rambo, C. (2013). Twitch: A performance of chronic liminality. In S. H. Jones, T. E. Adams, & C. E. Ellis (Eds.), *Handbook of autoethnography* (pp. 627–638). Left Coast Press.

Richardson, L. (2000). Evaluating ethnography. *Qualitative Inquiry, 6*(2), 253–255. https://doi.org/10.1177/107780040000600207

Richardson, L. (2005). Writing: A method of inquiry. In N. K. Denzin & Y. S. Lincoln (Eds.), *Handbook of qualitative research* (2nd ed., pp. 959–978). SAGE.

Ronai, C. R. (1995). Multiple reflections of child sex abuse: An argument for a layered account. *Journal of Contemporary Ethnography, 23*(4), 395–426. https://doi.org/10.1177/089124195023004001

Ryle, G. (1990). *Collected papers: Volume II. Collected Essays 1929–1968*. Hutchinson. (Original work published 1949)

Sartre, J.-P. (1958). *Being and nothingness* (H. E. Barnes, Trans.). Philosophical Library.

Schrag, C. O. (1986). *Communicative praxis and the space of subjectivity*. Indiana University Press.

Schrag, C. O. (1997). *The self after postmodernity*. Yale University Press.

Scott, J. A. (2019). Embracing the vulnerabilities and possibilities of storytelling, listening, and (re)creating identity with others. *Storytelling, Self, Society, 14*(2). https://digitalcommons.wayne.edu/storytelling/vol14/iss2/5

Scott, J. A., & Houtzer, H. (2018). She was here: Narrative research as resistance to the loss of 'culturally uncomfortable' identities. *Qualitative Inquiry, 24*(2), 134–150. https://doi.org/10.1177/1077800416684876

Searle, J. R. (1995). *The construction of social reality*. The Free Press.

Shotter, J. (1993). *Conversational realities: Constructing life through language.* SAGE.

Spry, T. (2011). *Body, paper, stage: Writing and performing autoethnography.* Left Coast Press.

Stewart, J. (1995). *Language as articulate contact: Toward a post-semiotic philosophy of communication.* SUNY Press.

Tillich, P. (1952). *The courage to be.* Yale University Press.

Tillmann, L. M. (2009). Ode to academic labor. *International Review of Qualitative Research, 2*(1), 61–66. https://doi.org/10.1525/irqr.2009.2.1.61

Tracy, S. J. (2010). Qualitative quality: Eight "big-tent" criteria for excellent qualitative research. *Qualitative Inquiry, 16*(10), 837–851. https://doi.org/10.1177/1077800410383121

Tracy, S. J. (2020). *Qualitative research methods: Collecting evidence, crafting analysis, communicating impact* (2nd ed.). Wiley-Blackwell.

Tullis, J. A. (2013). Self and others: Ethics in autoethnographic research. In S. H. Jones, T. E. Adams, & C. E. Ellis (Eds.), *Handbook of autoethnography* (pp. 244–261). Left Coast Press.

Van Maanen, J. (1988). *Tales of the field: On writing ethnography.* University of Chicago Press.

Weems, M. E. (2008). *Awake at the end: A Heights Arts poet laureate anthology.* Bottom Dog Press.

Wyatt, J. (2018). *Therapy, stand-up, and the gesture of writing: Towards creative-relational inquiry.* Routledge.

Wyatt, J., & Gale, K. (2013). Getting out of selves: An assemblage/ethnography? In S. H. Jones, T. E. Adams, & C. E. Ellis (Eds.), *Handbook of autoethnography* (pp. 300–312). Left Coast Press.

Yeats, W. B. (1996). *The collected poems of W. B. Yeats.* Scribner. (Original work published 1919)

Zemeckis, R. (Director). (1994). *Forrest Gump* [Film]. Wendy Finerman Productions.

Index

A

Accidental autoethnography, 51–52
"Accidental Dialogue" (Poulos), 61–62
Accidental Ethnography (Poulos), 5
action
    building sense of, 57, 62–63
    in compelling stories, 34
    in evocative writing, 53
Active listening, 22
Active self-reflexivity, 4
Active writing, 31–33
Adams, T. E., 4, 6
Aesthetic merit, in evaluating
    autoethnography, 74
Alexander, Bryant Keith, 70
American Psychological Association, 73
Analysis (coda), 57, 65–66
Andrew, Stephen, 76
Approach
    and methodological integrity of work, 76
    in writing-as-inquiry, 54
Artifacts, searching for, 27
Assumptions
    in autoethnographic writing process,
      34–37
    embedded in narrative, 76
Attending to passage of time, 57, 63
Attunement
    in accidental autoethnography, 52
    to emotional states, 22–23
    to engage participant observation,
      21–22
    to using writing as response to life, 41
    for writing dialogue, 61
    in writing good autoethnography, 29

Audience
    for arts-based research, 71
    knowing your, 57, 58
Autobiography, autoethnography vs., 5
Autoethnography (auto/ethnography;
    [auto]ethnography), 3–17
    accidental, 51–52
    as approach to living life, 32
    benefits of, 77–78
    collaborative, 71–72
    critical, 6, 68, 69
    defined, 4–5
    distinguishing features of, 16–17
    evaluating quality of, 74–76
    forms and structures of, 56
    as fundamentally disruptive, 77
    history of, 6–10
    layered accounts, 5, 68–69
    performance, 68–70
    philosophical and epistemological
      background of, 14–16
    pioneers in, 13–14
    poetic inquiry, 70–71
    in the qualitative tradition, 10–13
    qualities/characteristics of, 5, 12
    rationale for, 10–11
    as research, 3, 4
    rewards of, 77–78
    as social fiction, 71
    weaknesses of, 77
    writing. *See* Writing-as-inquiry;
      Writing process and practices
"An Autoethnography of Memory and
    Connection" (Poulos), 9–10

About the Author

Christopher N. Poulos, PhD, is professor (and former head) of communication studies at the University of North Carolina at Greensboro. He teaches courses in relational and family communication, ethnography, ethics, dialogue, and film. For his autoethnographic work on family grief and family stories, he won the Ellis-Bochner Autoethnography and Personal Narrative Research Award in 2007. His book, *Accidental Ethnography: An Inquiry Into Family Secrecy,* won the Best Book Award from the Ethnography Division of the National Communication Association in 2011. His work has appeared in *Qualitative Inquiry, Cultural Studies ↔ Critical Methodologies, Communication Theory, Southern Communication Journal, International Review of Qualitative Research, Qualitative Communication Research,* and many edited books. Dr. Poulos is a founding member of the International Congress of Qualitative Inquiry and former chair of the Communication Ethics and Ethnography Divisions of the National Communication Association.

About the Series Editors

Clara E. Hill, PhD, earned her doctorate at Southern Illinois University in 1974. She started her career in 1974 as an assistant professor in the Department of Psychology, University of Maryland, College Park, and is currently there as a professor.

She is the president-elect of the Society for the Advancement of Psychotherapy, and has been the president of the Society for Psychotherapy Research, the editor of the *Journal of Counseling Psychology*, and the editor of *Psychotherapy Research*.

Dr. Hill was awarded the Leona Tyler Award for Lifetime Achievement in Counseling Psychology from Division 17 (Society of Counseling Psychology) and the Distinguished Psychologist Award from Division 29 (Society for the Advancement of Psychotherapy) of the American Psychological Association, the Distinguished Research Career Award from the Society for Psychotherapy Research, and the Outstanding Lifetime Achievement Award from the Section on Counseling and Psychotherapy Process and Outcome Research of the Society for Counseling Psychology. Her major research interests are helping skills, psychotherapy process and outcome, training therapists, dream work, and qualitative research.

She has published more than 250 journal articles, 80 chapters in books, and 17 books (including *Therapist Techniques and Client Outcomes: Eight Cases of Brief Psychotherapy*; *Helping Skills: Facilitating Exploration, Insight, and Action*; and *Dream Work in Therapy: Facilitating Exploration, Insight, and Action*).

Sarah Knox, PhD, joined the faculty of Marquette University in 1999 and is a professor in the Department of Counselor Education and Counseling Psychology in the College of Education. She earned her doctorate at the University of Maryland and completed her predoctoral internship at The Ohio State University.

Dr. Knox's research has been published in a number of journals, including *The Counseling Psychologist*, *Counselling Psychology Quarterly*, *Journal of Counseling Psychology*, *Psychotherapy*, *Psychotherapy Research*, and *Training and Education in Professional Psychology*. Her publications focus on the psychotherapy process and relationship, supervision and training, and qualitative research. She has presented her research both nationally and internationally and has provided workshops on consensual qualitative research at both U.S. and international venues.

She currently serves as coeditor-in-chief of *Counselling Psychology Quarterly* and is also on the publication board of Division 29 (Society for the Advancement of Psychotherapy) of the American Psychological Association. Dr. Knox is a fellow of Division 17 (Society of Counseling Psychology) and Division 29 (Society for the Advancement of Psychotherapy) of the American Psychological Association.